WARM DEMANDER TEACHERS

WARM DEMANDER TEACHERS

Healthy, Whole, and Transformational

FRANITA WARE

FOR INFORMATION

Corwin
A Sage Company
2455 Teller Road
Thousand Oaks, California 91320
(800) 233-9936
www.corwin.com

Sage Publications Ltd.
1 Oliver's Yard
55 City Road
London EC1Y 1SP
United Kingdom

SAGE Publications India Pvt. Ltd.
Unit No 323-333, Third Floor, F-Block
International Trade Tower Nehru Place
New Delhi 110 019
India

SAGE Publications Asia-Pacific Pte. Ltd.
18 Cross Street #10-10/11/12
China Square Central
Singapore 048423

Vice President and
Editorial Director: Monica Eckman

Senior Acquisitions Editor: Megan Bedell

Senior Content Development
Editor: Mia Rodriguez

Project Editor: Amy Schroller

Copy Editor: Amy Hanquist Harris

Typesetter: C&M Digitals (P) Ltd.

Cover Designer: Gail Buschman

Marketing Manager: Melissa Duclos

Printed and bound by CPI Group (UK) Ltd, Croydon, CR0 4YY

Library of Congress Cataloging-in-Publication Data

Names: Ware, Franita, author.

Title: Warm demander teachers : healthy, whole, and transformational / Franita Ware.

Description: Thousand Oaks, California : Corwin, [2025] | Includes bibliographical references and index.

Identifiers: LCCN 2024033971 | ISBN 9781071928387 (paperback) | ISBN 9781071928394 (epub) | ISBN 9781071928400 (epub) | ISBN 9781071928417 (pdf)

Subjects: LCSH: Culturally relevant pedagogy—United States. | Effective teaching—United States. | African American students—Social conditions. | Teacher-student relationships—United States. | Teachers—Mental health—United States. | Multicultural education—United States.

Classification: LCC LC1099 .W38 2025 |
DDC 370.1170973—dc23/eng/20240913
LC record available at https://lccn.loc.gov/2024033971

This book is printed on acid-free paper.

24 25 26 27 28 10 9 8 7 6 5 4 3 2 1

Contents

Acknowledgments

Faith is the substance of things hoped for, the evidence of things not seen. (Hebrews, 11.1)

To the ancestors of the land on which this work was written, the Arapaho and Cheyenne. I am grateful to my Ancestors and the people who have influenced my thinking, shared love, faith, encouragement, and laughter.

To the first Dr. Ware, my sister-in-love, Melva Ware, PhD, and to Allegra Happy Haynes, Winifred R. Harris, Joy Harris, Hezekiah Harris, Ka'Tanya Harris, and my dad, Pastor King Harris. To my family the Wares, Griffins, Harrises, Johnsons, and Hayneses.

To Deidra A. Adams, Jena P. Jones, Veleria Tweechie O'Kelley, Tiffany I. Gardner, Melissa Mimi Muniz, Amalia Espinoza Salinas, Sia Y. Chandler, Patricia Ochoa Winkler, Sallie Boyles, Kayla Billman, Romanda L. M. Jefferson, and Iya Funlayo, PhD.

To Marcia Allen Owens, JD, PhD, who shared cultural humility.

To Sylvia A. Bookhardt, Michael K. Sykes, Sandra Just, and Wayman W. White, who supported Radical Self-Care.

To Angelicque Tucker Blackmon, PhD, who is largely responsible for this book being written.

To the many educators who gave me the opportunity to learn the history and contemporary application of Warm Demander pedagogy.

Finally, to Dan Alpert, Megan Bendel, and everyone at Corwin.

Publisher's Acknowledgments

Corwin gratefully acknowledges the contributions of the following reviewer:

Janet Crews
Coordinator of Professional Learning
School District of Clayton
Clayton, MO

About the Author

Franita Ware is the CEO of F Ware PhD Consulting LLC and a Qualitative Data Analysis Consultant with Innovative Learning Center LLC.

She is a member of the Board of Directors of Scholars Unlimited.

Through a collaboration with Dr. Robin Greene, Dr. Ellen Honeck, and Mrs. Imani Morning, Dr. Ware and her colleagues were awarded the Professional Learning Network Award from the National Association for Gifted Children for Culturally Responsive Gifted Education.

She is also a founding member of Sistagraphy, The Collective of African American Female Photographers.

Dr. Ware received her doctorate degree from Emory University. She attained her master of arts degree in Early Childhood Education and School Leadership credentials from Clark Atlanta University.

She began her education and her teaching career in Atlanta Public Schools.

Learn more about bringing Franita Ware to your school or district at https://www.franitawarephd.com.

An Invitation to Become a Warm Demander Teacher

1

I'm going to ask you a question that I'm sure you've been asked before.

Why Did You Become a Teacher?

Although I can't speak for everybody who chose to enter the K–12 education profession, I believe that you did so for very good reasons: You wanted to help children/students improve their lives and their communities through education, and in the process, make the world a better place.

You're not alone. In a 2015 research study (Heinz, 2015) on motivations for choosing teaching as a career, teachers representing 23 countries and five continents confirmed my suspicion: The majority entered the profession for altruistic reasons.

Next, I have a follow-up question:

Has Your Career in Education Met Your Expectations?

I hope you have experienced recurring joy with your students and the excitement of many well-received lessons, yet I have reason to believe that this may not be the case for many of my readers for a number of reasons. A recent McKinsey study (Bryant et al., 2023) found that the annual attrition rate for classroom teachers amounted to approximately 8% over the past 10 years. At schools designated for Title 1 funding, the rate is nearly double. While a proportion of attrition may be due to retirements, promotions, and lateral moves, between 2021 and 2022 the overall attrition rate rose by 17%. Moreover, 64% of 2022 attrition can be attributed to quitting. Further, the Institute of Educational Sciences (Taie et al., 2023) found the attrition rate for Asian teachers was 13%, for Black, African American teachers was 10%, and for Hispanic teachers, 6%. Collectively, the loss of these teachers impacts the schools and the students who lost a respected teacher who provided representation of their cultural or racial identity.

Clearly, the Covid-19 pandemic played a role in these increases. Aside from the challenge of shifting from in-person to online and hybrid teaching, many educators were simultaneously confronted with life-altering realities such as illness, death of family members, and reduction of income due to the job loss of a partner or other household contributors. And when teachers finally were able to resume face-to-face instruction, the faces they greeted were often those of students whose lives had also been turned upside down, many suffering from PTSD (post-traumatic stress disorder). It's no wonder that reported levels of teacher stress, burnout, and mental illness reached an all-time high during this period.

We know that teacher working conditions were problematic well before the pandemic. Poor compensation, long hours (an average of 53 hours each week), and a general lack of respect for the profession are longstanding problems (Walker, 2023). Public school teachers, in particular, are too often blamed by politicians and the media for a host of ills, many of which are products of misguided and inequitable policies that were imposed upon them by people with no understanding of teaching and learning, let alone the students they teach. And more recently, onerous state policies have sanctioned book bans and silenced critical examination of the harm caused by school policies specific to race, American history, and sexual and gender identities. This form of censorship not only severely limits teachers' academic freedom but is extremely harmful to students as well.

If you have ever experienced moments in which you feel frustrated, disparaged, lonely, or even wounded, take comfort in the fact that you are not alone. Many of us are sorely in need of healing, but all too often, what we get is toxic positivity and insincere reminders to "take care of yourselves (but please don't take a day off because we can't get a substitute)."

My intention is not to rub salt in a wound or discourage anybody from entering the field of education. I believe teaching is the noblest of professions—it is politically, spiritually, and personally rewarding, and teachers are some of the most brilliant, dedicated, and loving people I know. Many teachers have healed their own hearts and lives through caring for students and watching them succeed. We *need* excellent teachers more than ever! Let me offer some reassurance: In all likelihood, the "problem" isn't you, and it certainly isn't your students or their families. The problem is the system in which you work. And just to be clear, by "system" I'm not referring to your administration or your school district. I am referring to an education system that was never designed to serve the majority of our children in public schools.

If I haven't convinced you to stay in the profession, here's some additional reassurance: Emotional and physical hurt *can* be healed, and systems can be changed. The best part is that *you* can be part of that change.

In my career in education, I have listened to and learned from scholars, dedicated teachers, and school leaders who have disclosed not only their struggles but also their triumphs. I believe many, if not most, of you see quality education for our children as a moral and social justice imperative and a viable path of resistance to the systems designed to oppress communities. I believe that your intentions are honorable, and you share my heartfelt commitment to promote educational and racial equity and disrupt oppressive systems. Yet despite our goal to make education better, our education system is frequently unhealthy.

I want to create in our classrooms, schools, systems, and our profession a culture of health and humanity that is inclusive of all the people who work in the school and support students, but I can't do it without you. You and I can become the change. It's time to take steps to begin healing both teachers and students. In that spirit, consider this chapter a personal invitation: I invite you to start your journey to become a **Warm Demander Teacher**. This book seeks to provide the support you need to become a healthy, whole, and transformational educator.

Warm Demander Teachers ground their practice in high expectations for their students. But as I learned from my own research and practice, reversing the toxic effects of systemic racism and centuries of oppression takes more than holding high expectations. It also involves forming positive relationships with students that are grounded in trust and a finely honed awareness of the cultural nuances of relationships. When teachers establish such relationships, they can also lovingly nudge their students to take on increasing levels of academic challenge and, ultimately, take responsibility for their own learning. Warm Demander Teachers further promote student agency through frequent use of inquiry-based teaching strategies. The delicate dance between expressing our loving care *and* demanding excellence is the dynamic of Warm Demander teaching. And we master this dance by first looking closely within ourselves. My "choreography" rests on an important idea: In order to transform our systems, we must first transform ourselves through honest reflection, self-awareness, and self-healing.

While becoming a Warm Demander Teacher requires strength, courage, and perseverance, the rewards will astonish you. In addition to improving your relationships with your students and restoring your ideals about teaching to expand the lives of young people, imagine simply increasing the number of rewarding and even fun days where students are not only engaged but are active participants in their learning. And remind yourself that the promise of such days, the promise of watching your students soar, were the primary reasons that you made the choice to become a teacher.

I invite you to envision a new reality.

The Basis of This Book and Why I Wrote It

The first Warm Demander Teacher in my life was my mother, M. Frances Ware. I didn't know it at the time, but I now realize I was born into a Warm Demander style of mothering that was culturally consistent with my community and delivered a clear expectation for me to excel at life. My mother taught me through her actions and phenomenal creativity that our current reality is not a limitation if we choose to envision and work to create a new reality.

My mother was clear that my success in school was her unwavering expectation. Consistent with the loving reciprocity we see in Warm Demander Teacher/Student relationships, I wanted to achieve her high expectations so she would be proud of me. Fortunately, I was part of a stable school community with teachers who not only shared my mother's goal but also shared my cultural/racial identity (Howell et al., 2019). My teachers were, for the most part, committed and held high expectations for their students. We experienced loving reciprocity, the school embodied a strong sense of community, and students benefited from its high teacher-retention rate. My sixth-grade teacher, Mrs. Henson-Fulton, was an excellent Warm Demander Teacher who, later in life, introduced me to the teaching profession when she invited me to be a substitute teacher at the school where she served as the principal. In that environment, Warm Demander pedagogy was frequent and normalized. On my first, not-so-successful day as a substitute teacher, her feedback to me exemplified an honest Warm Demander perspective: "You're going to let kindergarteners run over you?"

Later, as a graduate student of Dr. Jacqueline Jordan Irvine, I was introduced to the article that would define my research, an article she coauthored on Warm Demanders (Irvine & Fraser, 1998). While the term *warm demander* initially appeared in articles by researcher Judith Kleinfeld (1975) and later, James Vasquez (1988), it was Dr. Irvine's article that resonated for me. The article explored the unique, culturally specific pedagogical style of African American teachers—a style that, at least at the time of Dr. Irvine's article publication, seemed incongruent with mainstream professional standards such as the National Board for Professional Teaching Standards. As I studied the article, I affectionately reflected on my prior Warm Demander Teachers. I was also struck by the realization that I was simultaneously learning from and experiencing Dr. Irvine as a Warm Demander Teacher. These realizations, combined with my own awareness of how I benefited from the efforts of my Warm Demander Teachers, sparked my desire to conduct further research into Warm Demander pedagogy.

I synthesized this research in a widely read paper published in a peer-reviewed journal in 2006 (Ware, 2006). My research methodology was qualitative, and my data were collected from interviews and hours of observations with two African American Warm Demander Teachers, Ms. Willis, a 30-year veteran teacher, and Mrs. Carter, who was in her sixth year of teaching at the time I conducted my research. Ms. Willis, an exemplary Warm Demander Teacher, taught in a building in the center of a low-income housing community. In the course of my observation, I was struck by the realization that her students were likely to have been labeled "at-risk" or judged as "deficient" by non-Warm Demander educators on the basis of their culture, race, and socioeconomic status. Like my sixth-grade teacher, Mrs. Henson-Fulton, Ms. Willis exemplified teachers who were influential, loving, and encouraging, while demanding nothing short of excellence. Her high expectations for academic growth and achievement served to help her students to reject the deficit narratives they were exposed to from anyone outside of their classroom, to rid themselves of internalized racism, and to believe in themselves despite external narratives (Foster, 1997; Walker, 1995, 2018). The style of teaching that I observed in both Ms. Willis's and Mrs. Carter's classroom fostered family-like relationships that served to build trust and motivate students to take on increasingly demanding challenges. Their students positively responded to their teachers' culturally nuanced, loving, and sometimes "fussy" demands to refocus on the academic materials and attain the expected intellectual rigor that the teachers expected and fully believed that they were capable of. Significantly, these teachers had a relationship with their students so that the fussy demands were interpreted as neither harmful nor traumatizing. Instead, it signaled the teachers' sincere beliefs that "they are too smart to be acting the way they are acting, or submitting the work they are turning in (or not turning in) . . . a belief in a child's ability to do better, that is the message that many children are eager to hear" (Delpit, 2012, p. 81).

These Warm Demander Teachers, by virtue of their shared, collectivist racial and cultural identities had a natural way of engaging with their students that built upon familial roles, culturally contextualized humor, warmth, and empowering care for students who needed support for their physical or academic needs. They also modeled their belief in the intrinsic value of their shared African heritage, a belief that inspired greatness. These complex relationships created loving reciprocity that welcomed demands for excellence from students who were supported by these empowered teachers.

My interest in Warm Demander pedagogy was far more than a research endeavor. My observations gave me a perspective on teaching that I, too, embraced when I taught college students at Spellman College, a Historically Black College for Women in Atlanta, Georgia. My relationship with these amazing students (some of whom were students at Morehouse College, a Historically Black College for Men) was synergistic: We respectively embraced culturally responsive, inquiry-based teaching and learning strategies. The pathway to this synergistic relationship was Warm Demander teaching, and collectively, we created a culture of achievement that is far from typical in many classrooms. Ultimately, they became exceptional, well-respected educators/scholars who appreciated Warm Demander teaching, but the benefits were reciprocal: They also made me a better teacher.

Further, my students helped me qualify and understand the less observable but significant traits of a Warm Demander Teacher. Long before it became a buzzword, my students and I touched briefly on the importance of self-care because, like James Baldwin (1963), I knew that teaching African American students was indeed a revolutionary act, and my students had to be healthy and whole to teach well. Many years passed before I understood that what is frequently identified as "self-care" often did not have the life-transforming effects of **Radical Self-Care**, a topic that is described in-depth in the following chapter. While developing workshops on Radical Self-Care, I came to understand what Audre Lorde (1988) was expressing when she stated, "Caring for myself is not self-indulgence, it is self-preservation, and that is an act of political warfare."

One of the benefits of being a lifelong learner and gaining new experience is that we cultivate a more insightful understanding of what we learned in the past. I now fully appreciate the efforts and influence of my Warm Demander Teachers, as well as the manner in which other writers and researchers have examined this unique form of pedagogy. This book is grounded in the principles of **Sankofa**—a word from the language of the Akan of Ghana—that tells us that we can "go back and get it" or we can learn from the past to build the future. I have looked back to those who contributed to the classical canon of culturally responsive teaching (Bartolomé, 2008; Delpit, 1995, 2006; Irvine, 1990, 2002; Ladson-Billings, 1994; Rolón-Dow, 2005; Walker, 1995, 2018) as well as more contemporary scholars who continue to build on this work and remind us that the journey is a lifelong endeavor (Emdin, 2016; Fergus, 2017; Hammond, 2015; Love, 2019, 2023; Muhammad, 2020, 2023; Singh, 2019; and Steele & Cohn-Vargas, 2013.)

Writing a book is both a leap of faith and a labor of love. I would be remiss in not acknowledging the influence of important scholars and authors who played essential roles in my decision to write this book. In her extensive body of brilliant scholarship, Jacqueline Jordan Irvine

(2002) introduced the genus of culturally responsive teachers who were complex and, most importantly, *whole* in her edited volume *In Seach of Wholeness: African American Teachers and Their Culturally Specific Classroom Practices*. Lisa Delpit, particularly in her transformational book *Multiplication Is for White People: Raising Expectations for Other People's Children* (2012), reawakened my desire to revisit this research with intentionality. Zaretta Hammond, who read my article and encouraged me to write this book, authored *Culturally Responsive Teaching and the Brain* (2015), another landmark work, and appreciated Warm Demander practices as pedagogy rather than classroom management. Finally, I continue to learn from the practitioners with whom I collaborate in my educational leadership and consulting work. I have learned from and been inspired by their journeys to Warm Demander practice, and from them, I have honed my understanding of both the catalysts and barriers to becoming healthy and whole.

The Guiding Principles of This Work

Before you begin your journey, I encourage you to familiarize yourself with some fundamental assumptions and principles that are foundational to my approach to Warm Demander Teaching.

#1: You can't heal others without first healing yourself.

The essence of reflective practice is learning from and responding to our own (and, in some cases, others') experiences. As I began to develop and deliver workshops on Warm Demander pedagogy, I came to realize that teacher behaviors that inspired student achievement that were the norm in my cultural/racial community were complex, and the teachers' actions were their positive response to the external stress of American schools. One of the things that I learned early on is that the high level of stress that is endemic to the American workplace—including our schools—is a barrier to engaging in the inner work that is prerequisite to becoming a Warm Demander Teacher. Similarly, when our brains continually revert to fight-or-flight mode, we are unlikely to form positive relationships with our students. But most importantly, stress at high levels, when left unchecked, can become an "occupational hazard," the consequences of which are fatigue, anxiety, sleeplessness, occupational burnout, disease, and, in the worst cases, death. This understanding led me to research and practice Radical Self-Care, which is now an integral part of my workshops and teachings on Warm Demander pedagogy. When you think about the word "radical," you may envision a dramatic and total transformation of yourself and everything you do, but it's the opposite; instead, think about taking small, consistent, and sustainable actions that lead to much larger and observable improvements in physical, emotional, and brain health. What makes it "radical" is that in doing so we reject an oppressive culture that values stress and embrace the habits and beliefs that heal ourselves and our students.

#2: Warm Demander pedagogy is more than a bag of tricks; it begins with our own self-awareness.

If you are a seasoned teacher, you've probably heard about the latest silver-bullet curriculum, instructional framework, or teaching strategy that will engage your students, accelerate their learning, wash your car, and change your life! After being exposed to such promises or pitches, you may even have a healthy degree of cynicism. The dominant culture of our schools and society favors quick fixes and simplistic cause-and-effect reasoning over deep reflection and complexity. If nothing else, you've learned that teaching and learning are highly complex endeavors. What I've learned is that, especially when you and your students don't share common racial or cultural identities, you not only have to cultivate a deep knowledge of your students, but you have to know yourself, your purpose, and motivation for teaching—inner work that carries its own complexity.

For this reason, the theory of action that informs this book is that a deeper knowledge of ourselves as educators and humans will make us more effective practitioners of Warm Demander pedagogy. The "inner work" that is the subject matter of subsequent chapters, including exploring our beliefs, biases, and cultural/racial identities, is essential to forming the relationships that are at the heart of Warm Demander teaching. For most of us, the journey comes with a fair amount of emotional labor, cognitive dissonance, and occasional discomfort. It also is a lifelong endeavor, but again, the rewards, including enhanced job satisfaction, improved relationships with your students and peers, increased student agency, and your own restored health and wholeness, are immeasurable.

#3: Self-knowledge is great, but will it make me a better teacher?

The brief answer is yes, but I also appreciate the need to connect the self-discovery process to one's own decisions and actions as a teacher. For this reason, I've sought to close "knowing-doing" gaps by exploring how understanding ourselves, our students, and the systems in which we live and work relate to Warm Demander pedagogy. In most cases, I accomplish this through providing opportunities for the reader to engage in reflective practice (Cadray, 1999) by providing examples of the process of forming new beliefs that inform Warm Demander practices, decisions, and moves.

#4: With enhanced self-knowledge comes cultural humility.

As we become more self-aware, we gain a greater understanding of how our lived experiences, beliefs, and cultures are alike or different from those of our students. One of the ways in which our education system has failed to serve *all* our student populations is by not acknowledging the inherent strengths and cultural wealth of these children and their families. Cultural humility (Tervalon & Murray-Garcia, 1998) combines self-knowledge with curiosity and a willingness to listen to and learn from others. In doing so, we are aware of our own biases and how they can contribute to deficit-based and judgmental thinking. Instead, we gain both an appreciation for and knowledge of our students that supports our high expectations of them. Learning to listen humbly to and learn from our students and their community is an essential prerequisite to Warm Demander teaching.

#5: You can become a Warm Demander Teacher without sharing the cultural and racial identities of your students.

I had my own biases initially, but as I continued to engage in professional development with teachers, I had to expand my beliefs and hope, especially after I met teachers who *willingly* embraced the internal work become Warm Demander Teachers. My research, as well as that of my graduate school professor, Dr. Irvine, explored the exemplary practices of Black teachers who taught Black students. Yet Dr. Irvine always emphasized that *all teachers could be Warm Demander Teachers*. I've come to understand that it requires a deeper level of introspection, learning, and, of course, cultural humility, *and* it is within your reach, even if you don't share common backgrounds and cultural nuances with your students. It may take some time to establish a level of trust with BIPOC[1] students who don't look like you, but as you begin to understand the historical and sociocultural reasons for their hesitation, you will gradually appreciate earning their trust. The framework that I share in this book can support *all* teachers on the journey and has had a proven impact on practice, based on the feedback I have received from teachers and educational leaders.

#6: Although my research focused on African American teachers and students, Warm Demander pedagogy benefits all BIPOC student groups.

As in my 2006 article, this book includes a number of examples and quotes from Black, African American Warm Demander Teachers who are primarily responsible for Black, African American, and other identities of students. I focused on this group of educators for several reasons:

(1) As I shared previously, my own Warm Demander Teachers had a tremendous positive impact on me, yet Black, African American teachers make up a small portion of our nation's teaching force and they are typically undervalued by their schools as well as researchers and the media. While I remain hopeful that this will change, I believe that an acknowledgement of their gifts, skills, and accomplishments is long overdue. Moreover, I believe that teachers who don't identify as Black or African American can learn a great deal by listening and learning from them and how they have humanized Black, African American students (Howell et al., 2019).

(2) Since I share the racial and cultural identities of these teachers and their students, consequently, I'm most comfortable writing about them. In contrast, I don't think I can fairly or accurately capture the experiences or cultural nuances of other BIPOC communities.

[1]BIPOC is an acronym used in the United States that means Black, Indigenous, and People of Color. While some argue that the term is problematic in that it blurs the distinctions between each group's histories and cultures, I use it as a form of shorthand in the context of this book. What these groups have in common are histories of discrimination and marginalization that have endured across generations and into the present, as evidenced by the deficit narratives about children that pervade our schools.

With that said, I've seen evidence in both research and practice that Warm Demander pedagogy benefits *all* students—especially BIPOC students. We can acknowledge the important differences between the cultures and histories of these populations while, at the same time, acknowledging some important commonalities: Not only do they share common histories of systemic oppression, discrimination, and marginalization, but many of them are also members of collectivist cultures.

An early example of research that explored aspects of Warm Demander pedagogy (long before the term was coined) with a racial/ethnic student population comes from Kleinfeld (1975), who studied Alaskan Indigenous teachers and students. Warm Demander Teachers who participated in this study demonstrated belief in students' success and rejected deficit beliefs and about them. Examples of their behaviors are consistent with the canon of classic literature on culturally responsive teaching (Delpit, 1995, 2006; Foster, 1997; Irvine, 1990, 2002; Irvine & Armento, 2001; Irvine & Fraser, 1998; Ladson-Billings, 1994; Rolón-Dow, 2005; and Walker, 1995, 2018). Warm Demander Teachers also enjoyed their students and classroom interactions. The loving synergy created between students and teachers improved everyone's lives. Similarly, Schhneider et al. (2006) concluded that, consistent with all students, Hispanic students benefit from teachers who build upon personal relationships to encourage academic achievement through high expectations for students growth. If you are familiar with the work and legacy of the late Jaime Escalante, who taught math to low-income, Latinx students at Garfield High in East Los Angeles, you already have a sense of what Warm Demander pedagogy "looks like." While nobody believed that Escalante's students were capable of learning high-level mathematics (or anything, for that matter), Escalante and his students proved them wrong. Not only did they learn calculus, but many achieved high scores on the challenging AP exam. Portrayed by Edward James Olmos in the 1988 film *Stand and Deliver,* Escalante demanded nothing short of excellence from his students. He also continually affirmed their cultural identities as well as their learner identities by reminding them that it was the Mayans who gave us the concept of zero.

Prior to the *Stand and Deliver* film, Hollins (1982) published the article "The Marva Collins Story Revisited: Implications for Regular Classroom Instructions." Collins's instructional strategies were identified to be culturally congruent, building upon interaction patterns found in traditional Black family and church culture. In her class, competition was minimalized, and students worked in cooperative or complementary dyads or triads. Strategies that are also found in Warm Demander teaching, Hollins noted that "good teaching that was displayed in the Marva Collins story may appear obvious. There was good discipline, high motivation, high teacher expectation, positive reinforcement, adequate/quality time on task, well-organized curriculum, and genuine concern for children" (p. 39).

Additionally, Marva Collins' pedagogy was presented in the 1981 television film titled *The Marva Collins Story*. As the founder of the Westside Preparatory School in Chicago Garfield Park in 1975, Collins's success was documented in a 1977 article in *The Chicago Sun-Times* and a 1995 *60 Minutes* interview.

While there is ample research to support these guiding principles, there is nothing like the evidence from one's own practice. The framework I have developed to support all teachers on their personal journey has had a proven impact in my professional development sessions, based on the feedback I have received from teachers and educational leaders. Moreover, throughout you'll find quotes from teachers who've shared their journey and who will inspire you to embark on your own journey.

Are You Ready to Do *This* Work?

This book is not "one more thing" for you to do or another examination of equity and bias training. The contents will not be completed and forgotten by winter break. Instead, it is a guide that serves to spark a continuing process of reflection and growth. While I call upon my readers to face some uncomfortable truths, my intent is not to oppress or shame teachers. To the contrary, I believe in the power of excellent teaching, and I also believe that deficit thinking about the profession, teachers, and students ultimately harms everyone. Warm Demander Teachers engage in acts of multiple acts of liberation. First, they liberate themselves from the American ideal that overwhelming stress is a healthy environment in which to live and work. As they engage in Radical Self-Care and experience the long-term health benefits, Warm Demander Teachers can better engage in critical analyses of their areas of growth and the schools in which they teach. I've seen the contents of this book, when applied with intentionality, as having the potential to be transformative.

If you have a sincere desire to return to the ideals that brought you into the teaching profession to begin with, I believe you *are* ready for this work. If you think of yourself as a lifelong learner, you are absolutely ready for this book. Warm Demander Teachers have historically been excited to explore new ways of thinking about instruction and are open to examining the realities of race as a variable of how students experience schools and their teachers. These teachers *willingly* discuss students' and their own cultural/racial identity as one element in the success of the relationship, as well as their perceptions of safety and the academic and leadership development of students. They realize that classrooms are not race-neutral and that colorblindness is a harmful myth. They understand that the educational debt that is owed to the children who have systematically been denied access to high-quality education by a system that is inequitable by design is enormous (Ladson-Billings, 2006). They also understand their unique role in reframing a new reality that is characterized by justice, healing, and love. And they reject the idea of "other people's children" (Delpit, 1995, 2006) and embrace "our children," which they demonstrate every day in their authentic relationships with students through loving reciprocity.

Gholdy Muhammad (2020), one of our leading education visionaries, examined the othering of students by teachers who referred to students as "my students" and then made disparaging comments about their students. Muhammad wonders "why are we still 'othering' children?" (p. 65). More than 40 years ago, James Baldwin (1980) solidified collective responsibility when he wrote, "The children are always ours, every single one of them, all over the globe." I believe that when we engage as a collective community and see our students' worth, we then will take responsibility for their progress. As such, the children/students in this book will be lovingly referred to as "our students," and I invite you to engage in collective responsibility for their growth.

A Brief Walk-Through of This Book

Systemic racism and intersecting systems of oppression disproportionately harm communities throughout the United States and globally, but *all* of us suffer their consequences. Healing from the toxic effects of an inequitable educational system is another important theme of this book, but as I've already stated, we can't begin healing others without first healing ourselves. For this reason, the journey to becoming a Warm Demander Teacher begins with a deep dive into Radical Self-Care—the subject matter of Chapter 2. As the journey unfolds in subsequent chapters, I offer repeated reminders to draw upon your Radical Self-Care practices as needed. Another "radical" aspect is recognizing the unanticipated health benefits through consistent implementation of Radical Self-Care practices. The work of challenging our deep-seated beliefs and biases, unpacking whiteness, and confronting our own fears can be emotionally taxing and even triggering. Through my own educational leadership and consulting practice, I've learned that in the absence of a Radical Self-Care toolbox, few are able to complete the journey. I cannot stress its importance enough.

Chapter 3 begins the journey into self-knowledge with some fundamental concepts that create Warm Demander pedagogy, including coming to terms with interrupting our biases, practicing cultural humility, and recognizing our own power and authority as educators. Further, this understanding can be directed toward the good of our students, through learning to practice critical care—a form of caring that honors students' identities and interrupts systems of oppression.

The journey continues in Chapter 4, which begins by unpacking whiteness—an essential concept that is frequently misrepresented and misunderstood but one that helps us to critically analyze the norms and practices of our classrooms, schools, education systems, and society at large. We then take a deep dive into cultural/racial identity—both our own and those of our students. Again, this understanding is foundational to the work of Warm Demander Teachers, who must first work to develop their own healthy cultural/racial identities before helping their students do the same. Related to this is the formation of positive *learner* identities in our students to counter the effects of stereotype threat and deficit assumptions. The chapter also touches on intersectionality—since teachers and students alike share multiple identities that are impacted by systems of oppression apart from race. Finally, we unpack the components of Warm Demander Teacher identities. Throughout Chapters 3 and 4, I have included practical examples of how these foundational concepts inform our pedagogical practice.

Chapter 5 provides a closer look at Warm Demander pedagogical practices through the voices of two highly effective Warm Demander Teachers. In addition to illustrating concepts discussed in prior chapters, *culturally responsive inquiry* is introduced as a Warm Demander teaching methodology that promotes higher levels of engagement, enhances critical thinking capacity, and promotes creativity, while simultaneously affirming student identity.

Finally, Chapter 6 returns to the theme of healing from the harm caused by an inequitable, dehumanizing system. Both educators and students have been harmed by the deficit narratives that have supported diminished expectations, erosion of student–learner identities, and what scholar and author Bettina Love calls "spirit murdering" (2019). We can and must work collectively with all members of the school community to promote cultures of healing and inclusivity.

In conclusion, I want to reaffirm my belief that such harms are reparable and that healing begins with you! To be sure, healing is hard work that requires you to reject false narratives about students, teachers, and their communities that are engrained in our policies and practices. You may be the one teacher who initiates the change, but rest assured, the goal is achievable, one school community at a time.

Let's begin the journey together!

Facilitator Guide

Encourage participants to create a journal to document their experiences and reflections from the professional development experiences of the book.

- What are your feelings about teaching?
- Do you have colleagues and friends who have decided to leave teaching?
  - What do you believe is needed to retain and recruit teachers?
- What are your beliefs about Warm Demander Teachers?
- Have you experienced a Warm Demander Teacher relationship?
  - Analyze what made them Warm Demanders.
- Are you open to new ideas about your ability to be a Warm Demander Teacher, your relationship with your students and their ability to be successful, and the healing of your school community?
- What are your initial ideas on how to identify a Warm Demander Teacher?

Radical Self-Care

2

> *Caring for myself is not self-indulgence. It is self-preservation, and that is an act of political warfare.*
>
> **—Audre Lorde**

American culture is steeped in excess stress. Stop and think of the stress you experienced today simply from tuning into the news. Chances are you learned of the latest episode of social injustice, alarming evidence of our climate crisis, or any number of catastrophes on the national or global fronts. The frequency and ease with which you can access the latest news is but one source of our stress.

Reflection

Allow yourself to stop and take a calming breath. As you pause, think of your values and views of the world.

- How are you?
- How is your life going?
- Do you have strategies and practices in place to manage stress and to build your health?

Now think of how externally induced stress, like that that accompanies the nightly news, touches you personally:

- What are the stressors in your personal life?
- What are they in your professional life?

(Continued)

(Continued)

- Do you (as many people do) conflate your professional stress as some sort of validation of your professional achievement, success, and importance?
- Do you need to be told to rest (Hersey, 2022; Riley, 2024)?

A toxic combination of traumatic experiences has contributed to unprecedented levels of stress in much of the world. While many of us experience digital devices and emerging technology as marvelous assets in our daily lives, there is no question that they compound stress in both our personal and professional spheres, Moreover, the stress experienced during the coronavirus pandemic has not dissipated in its endemic aftermath.

Think about this: In some ways, we live in a culture that values stress. It's no wonder that personal neglect has also become an epidemic. Yoga, meditation, mindfulness training, vigorous exercise, ice cream, and even prescription medication may help you in the short term, but none of these are panaceas for an out-of-balance world. More than ever, we need Radical Self-Care.

The Author Reflects

I knew my professional life was stressful, but I believed I was managing the pressure. To relax, I engaged in quiet evenings and scented candles, occasional walks, lots of manicures, and glasses of wine. I did not realize that I was following the media-driven myth of self-care and not engaging in what I now know to be impactful self-care strategies that contribute to restoration and health.

After months of misguidedly managed professional stress, I was exhausted, experiencing brain fog, and had normalized living on less than six hours of restless sleep. I finally became fatigued and lethargic. I had hit a wall and knew I was not physically healthy. While I was thinking of how to regain my health, I remember saying, "I've got to do something radical to get out of this." The idea of Radical Self-Care started to emerge. My own unmanaged stress, diminished creativity, and forced productivity are what led me to create Radical Self-Care in 2016.

Up until this point, I'd always prided myself on my ability to take care of myself. I encouraged teachers and my students to practice routines and rituals that I believed to be self-care. I was in for a surprise. When I sought to develop what became the Radical Self-Care workshop, I learned from my research that what I thought was effective was not. Nor was it sustainable. It would not move the needle from barely surviving to thriving. Those superficial self-care strategies were hardly radical, nor could they create a foundation of health. It may seem paradoxical, but part of Radical Self-Care involves shifting our mindset from the idea that we must make major (or "radical") changes to one that values establishing and meeting small goals of impactful self-care. These small but impactful moves naturally create changes in our brains that are, indeed, radical. They, in turn, lead to greater happiness and a natural evolution of growth and increased health (Achor, 2010; Chatterjee, 2018a, 20018b; Hersey, 2022; Suzuki, 2017; Thurett, 2015).

When I hit the wall, I was experiencing burnout, brain fog, forgetfulness, fatigue, anxiety, poor sleep (either interrupted or less than six hours), weight gain and body aches, tension in relationships, the feeling that I was overwhelmed by life and responsibility, and compassion fatigue. Ultimately, I said, "This workload is not sustainable." I thought I was having a unique experience with that long list of woes, but when I started facilitating the Radical Self-Care workshop to educators, I found most of the people who attended had or were currently experiencing most or all the same symptoms.

Barely Surviving

Compassion fatigue is significant for educators, especially as we see record numbers of teachers leaving the profession. Not only does this condition deplete our energy, but it also diminishes our desire to work as an effective teacher and change agent. Think about it: It's hard to imagine taking the time to critically analyze how to interrupt systems of oppression in public education when we can barely get ourselves out of bed in the morning. Finally, as might be expected, it keeps us from doing exactly what would renew us both personally and professionally: becoming Warm Demander Teachers. Educator exhaustion and compassion fatigue support systems of oppression. The idea that the workload is unsustainable—a common and frequently realistic complaint for teachers—leads to burnout and the continued oppression of our students and educators through the loss of critical examination of policies and decisions. Leaving the profession, an increasingly frequent decision among teachers who genuinely want to support their students, is another consequence. We can't expect educators with increasingly demanding workloads and high levels of stress to have enough resilience to interrupt systems of oppression and implicit bias through transformational instruction, as well as to serve as advocates for their students, even if they have the desire to do so. However, we do have the means to support teachers to effectively meet challenges and create a culture of Radical Self-Care—a very attainable goal.

Cultivating awareness is the first step toward creating a Radical Self-Care culture. I lacked such an awareness when I believed that superficial self-care "quick fixes" like scented candles were enough to keep me from hitting a wall. With time, I became aware of what I lacked: long-term and consistent strategies for effective self-care. I also wasn't aware of how vulnerable I had become to unmanaged stress, health crises, diminished work productivity, and tensions in my relationships. When toxic conditions are normalized, we lose sight of the possibility of a new normal. In the same way, teachers must first become aware of what they are missing and how the absence of Radical Self-Care is harming them. Schools and teams that work to build a culture that values Radical Self-Care have documented progressive gains in health, personal resilience, productivity, and enhanced relationships with students. School cultures that value self-care are supported by communities that intentionally collaborate to minimize teachers' "personal stress threshold" (Chatterjee, 2018a). Working conditions improve, as do teachers' physical, emotional, and brain health. Further, classroom and school cultures improve, easing the ability to implement disruption of biases. Removing such biases furthers Warm Demander Teacher relationships and pedagogy. Notably, educators who practiced Radical Self-Care before the coronavirus pandemic and virtual learning period reported possessing the required resilience to navigate through the ambiguous educational context.

Radical Self-Care is the rejection of American culture that values stress as a byproduct of success and importance. It also rejects the January 1st resolution mindset that to fix your life or health you must engage in an overly ambitious reconstruction of your current habits and practices. Radical Self-Care values the belief that Rest is Resistance (Hersey, 2022), and relaxation must be intentional and on our schedule every day to create the restoration we need (Chatterjee, 2018b). It is amazing to me that it is *radical* to be intentional about our health and reject stressing ourselves and matching the chaotic energy we see in schools and society to the detriment of our physical and brain health. Finally, Radical Self-Care is based on taking small, consistent, and sustainable actions that lead to much larger and unanticipated health transformations when practiced consistently. I have learned that it's not big changes that improve our lives and classrooms; it is the small changes that are implemented consistently. Think of a healthy classroom culture that is based on that premise. Fortunately, the self-care literature is significantly more accessible, and these ideas are less radical than when I wrote this training in 2016. The pandemic made these ideas mainstream. Yet, I see schools continue to embrace a stressful culture.

This chapter explains the need for Radical Self-Care as a strategy to interrupt the harmful effects of unmanaged stress or benign neglect of physical, emotional, or brain health for educators who need or want to expand their well-being for their own needs and to engage in the work in the following chapters. Further, through exploring sources of stress and their observable effects, educators can implement Radical Self-Care that leads to ongoing self-care. Such behaviors improve physical and emotional health, which leads to improved relationships and creates optimum conditions for becoming a Warm Demander Teacher.

Ah-h-h, Breathe

Let's stop and notice our breathing. Are you stressed just reading about stress? You can put your hand on your chest and slow your breathing by counting to 3 to inhale, then hold for 4, and exhale for 5. Do that activity until you feel relaxed. When your exhale is longer, that activates your relaxation mode (Chatterjee, 2018b).

Graphic source: istock.com/Skarin

Feeling more relaxed? Your yoga teacher got it right: It all starts with breathing. Chatterjee (2018b) identifies a focus on breathing and control of breath as an effective means to help control the release of cortisol, a hormone that is produced by the amygdala (a section of the brain that is linked to our emotions). While cortisol serves an important regulatory function in our bodies, excessive cortisol can cause a range of problems, including anxiety, depression, and even heart disease. Overproduction of cortisol—or what is often referred to as the "amygdala hijack" (Goleman, 1998, 2011)—can invoke a fight-or-flight response, which, as you might imagine, is not the best way to approach a classroom full of students on a Monday morning. Certainly, teaching can be a source of stress, and for some, cortisol overload can become an occupational hazard.

Oberle and Schonert-Reichel's (2016) researched the effects of occupational stress and burnout on teachers and the harm to teachers and students. One example is stress contagion, where stress can spill over from one individual to the next in a classroom. There is a synergistic relationship between teachers' and students' stressful experiences called a burnout cascade, which contributes to more reactive and punitive responses to classroom management. The researchers found that teacher burnout was predictive of the students' morning cortisol levels, and stressors in the school environment increased the cortisol levels. In those class environments, the teacher's lack of well-being, which is often related to a lack of support and resources, creates a reactive climate where the discipline of students is the focus, not rigorous and engaged instruction, and frustration is observable.

So what does all this have to do with breathing? It stands to reason that teachers with elevated levels of stress are unlikely to become Warm Demanders without first learning to slow down their cortisol production. Again, it all starts with breathing, and there is a neuroscientific reason for this. Sustained breathing will shift the control of our emotions and behaviors from the amygdala (the "emotional brain") to the prefrontal cortex (the rational brain).

Identify Your Stressors

Think of that little irritating jolt of shock experienced by static electricity. While irritating, the shock is small and manageable. A micro-stress dose (Chatterjee, 2018a) is comparable to a little dose of static electricity. One is an annoyance; multiple, frequent doses can make you irritable and stressed, impacting your overall health through a lack of stress management. A lot of micro-stressors can create emotional responses that may appear excessive.

Micro-stressors can begin before you even start your day. For instance, when you are awakened by a loud noise, you begin your day with a little jolt of stress. Multiple micro-stressors can start with your morning routine, commute, or preparation for teaching. If you have physical challenges, the simple acts of getting out of bed and dressing can deliver multiple doses of stress. The configuration of your home, obstacles to dress, bad-hair mornings, preparations to have a cup of coffee, the "what's for breakfast" question by your family or partner—they all can become micro-stressors, and all can occur before you begin your morning to teach.

Micro-stressors add to the observable stresses of teaching: lesson plans, test preparation, and the dissonance you may feel when working with students whose cultures are different from yours. Likewise, consider that your students are experiencing micro-stressors and trauma over which they have no control, such as the stress of daily racialized microaggressions, racial inequity, and systems of oppression in public education. Many of our students have significantly higher stress levels than the adults with whom they interact in a school environment.

> *Wellbeing is an act of resistance.*
>
> **—bell hooks**

Radical Self-Care starts with identifying and managing as many micro-stressors as possible. To contribute to your feeling of balance and control, you need to mitigate the impact of stress that contributes to your personal stress threshold (Chatterjee, 2018a). Identifying your stressors can make the difference between starting your day with anxiety or calmness. Teachers who are aware of their stress can begin the day by leading their class in breathing strategies and providing a sincere oxytocin boost/welcome to students, inviting them to a day of mentally rigorous and emotionally calming learning, shared compassion, and care. The sincere oxytocin welcome for both you and your students is foundational to creating a Warm Demander classroom.

> *I'm a better teacher because of Radical Self-Care.*
>
> **—Ms. Jones**

The Steps of Radical Self-Care

The first step of Radical Self-Care pertains to the intentional, ongoing care that is required to recover from physical, emotional, or brain health that resulted from extended neglect. Radical Self-Care becomes intentional, ongoing self-care through implementing **consistent small steps**, or bite-sized (Chatterjee/Suzuki, 2023) health habits that support neuroplasticity (or changes in the brain that happen from experiences)—in other words, connecting new neurons and making healthy habits stick.

The second step of Radical Self Care is a natural outcome of the first step. The positive **brain plasticity** (Chatterjee/Suzuki, 2023) that is an outcome of forming new neuron connections (Achor, 2010) accelerates your ability to overcome the fears and doubts that have held you back from achieving your goals. Think of the times you've heard, "I'd love to give up donuts, but they are always in the teacher's lounge!" Beneath this statement is a kind of learned helplessness that stems from the doubt or fear that the donut lover cannot possibly control their health. I have encountered similar doubts from stressed-out teachers who have yet to be exposed to the Radical Self Care concept. Think about it: Just as helplessness can be learned, so too can we learn to effectively manage our stress and engage in positive change. In fact, qualitative data shows that after attending Radical Self-Care workshops, participants report positive changes in their behavior. They learn that their actions do matter, and that sense of control leads to more positive behaviors (Achor, 2010).

The third step of Radical Self-Care can only be reached after the first two steps are implemented. It manifests as what some would deem a radical idea: **Through ongoing self-care, educators can become more equitable in their interactions with students and colleagues and therefore more easily and effectively navigate the anti-bias work to become a Warm Demander Teacher.** Think of it this way: For many of us, overcoming the barriers to equity—especially those that live within us in the form of biases—is much like overcoming the allure of the donuts in the teachers' lounge. The more we feel that we have some control in the matter, beginning with taking charge of our own health and well-being, the more freedom we have to shed the baggage that impedes our growth. As with the breathing exercises we do with our students every morning, the entire learning community will benefit.

A Metaphor: Take the Time to Recharge Your Battery

Remember the last time you looked at your phone and saw the thin red line that indicated you had exhausted the battery? Despite connecting your device to a charger, you experienced a delay before a minimal amount of charge allowed you to use it. Now, remember the last time you asked someone, including a stranger, to loan you a charger? It wasn't easy, but your own sense of urgency forced you to overcome your hesitation. Do we give ourselves the same sense of urgency to prevent our human battery from completely losing its charge that we give to caring for our phones? The depleted battery icon is a great representation of the need for Radical Self-Care because it demonstrates the energy available to you, your students, and your responsibilities to the people you care about. In some ways, teacher burnout is akin to an exhausted battery. Don't wait for it to happen—seek Radical Self-Care. NOW.

Graphic source: istock.com/YoGinta

Five Areas of Focus for Radical Self-Care

Radical Self-Care identifies five significant areas of focus to bring you into homeostasis so you can effectively address the challenges of being a Warm Demander educator: movement/exercise, nutrition, sleep, nurturing relationships, and purposeful work. Two additional areas that warrant your personal attention are faith/spirituality and financial health.

The theoretical framework of Radical Self-Care is based on Shawn Achor's work on Positive Psychology, and the study of neurogenesis and brain plasticity (Achor, 2010; Chatterjee, 2018a, 2018b; Chatterjee/Suzuki, 2023; Suzuki, 2017; Thurett, 2015). Similar to the first steps of Radical Self-Care described earlier, the science of Positive Psychology recommends focusing on one area of growth at a time and taking small, attainable steps. The success of those steps will maximize brain plasticity; the brain will naturally build upon prior successes and identify the next level of goals to continue to increase the individual's personal health.

As you read the next section, take time to reflect on the one area of focus you will implement. Although the word "radical" may suggest otherwise,

Radical Self-Care does not propose overwhelming and drastic improvements to your health all at once. Just ask anybody who has attempted to go on a strict diet while giving up smoking and starting a new job. Unfortunately, drastic changes frequently fail, and failure reinforces the belief that you cannot make significant improvements. Therefore, brain science overwhelmingly suggests that small, but sustainable positive changes lead to far more significant changes over time.

Participants in Radical Self-Care workshops who adhered to this principle have experienced significant success—success that they never would have imagined possible prior to engaging in the steps of Radical Self-Care. Over the long term, as educators progressed to addressing increasingly challenging aspects of their health, they were able to confront their most serious challenges. For example, one educator began Radical Self-Care by making dietary changes and, in the process, progressed to gaining deeper emotional perspectives on her relationships with other people, culminating in the realization she had overlooked her emotional needs. She later reported that by engaging in the process of Radical Self-Care she was able to address her sobriety.

The author Oludara Adeeyo (2022) also writes about radical self-care in her book *Self-Care for Black Women*:

> Knowing when you need to use radical self-care is essential to your wellness. The answer? Every day. What makes radical self-care so different from other types of self-care is that it requires you to give your full attention to your well-being. (p. 15)

Movement/Exercise

Suzuki (2017) and Thurett's (2015) TED Talks presented their research on the impact of exercise and brain health. Suzuki states that movement/exercise is the most important thing that you can do for your overall health. "Every time you move your body . . . starting with walking, your brain releases neurochemicals that make you feel good, . . . bringing your energy up, . . . the functions of your prefrontal cortex get sharper and if you do it in the morning it becomes habit forming" (Chatterjee/Suzuki, 2023).

Graphic source: istock.com/TuracNovruzova

Thurett points out that neurogenesis occurs through exercise and creates an improvement in mood, focus, and mental decline related to aging and stress. The belief that the only workouts that have a significant impact on your health are high-intensity and sweat-inducing is a myth. With the availability of digital devices that monitor ***movement***, teachers can be more cognizant of the extent of their movement and feel positive about it. Some may be surprised by the number of steps or movements that a teacher can attain during a workday. I encourage you to check in with your feelings after you've walked or jogged through your building or parking lot to attend a meeting. If you feel refreshed, was it the movement that led you to feeling healthier? If you still feel stressed, don't give up. Eventually, you will start to notice when movement helps to relieve your stress. The more relief you feel, the more you will make room for these opportunities in your day.

Attending to your physical well-being doesn't need to be complicated, stress-inducing, or expensive. For those who are able-bodied, walking is a straightforward and healthy way to exercise. Try increasing the amount of time you move by 10 minutes at a time either by increasing your walking or taking stairs more often (Chatterjee, 2018a). Movement with gradual and consistent increases creates the release of endorphins and dopamine—the "feel-good" hormones. If walking from the classroom to the cafeteria or other parts of the building isn't enough to help you feel these positive effects, you may want to look for additional opportunities to move outside of your campus in a more relaxing environment.

Those who choose movement as their focal point in enacting Radical Self Care should frequently reflect on their exercise practice by (1) examining if they should decrease or increase their exercise levels or change the activities that they engage in or (2) change their perspective from treating exercise as one more task to complete to seeing it as a joyful experience. And of course, teachers with physical or mobility concerns should follow the advice of their doctors or physical therapists on how to exercise in safe ways that enhances well-being.

In summary, sustained, intentional movement contributes to a reduction in stress and cortisol production while increasing the release of dopamine and endorphins—the feel-good hormones that send a signal to the brain that you are safe and not experiencing a hijacked amygdala. Living in a constant state of stress or having a high personal stress threshold hampers the ability to engage and enjoy life. In your professional life,

(Continued)

(Continued)

when the stress of teaching reaches unhealthy levels, your ability to engage with students as a Warm Demander is impaired.

Pampering activities such as bubble baths and long showers *enhance but do not replace* the small and consistent actions of Radical Self-Care to transform your health. In Wallace J. Nichols's (2014) book *Blue Mind*, he identifies the optimum state of health and healing as "blue mind," and it occurs when being near or immersed in large bodies of water. Baths and showers can help create the relaxed, healed, and creative state of blue mind. However, quick fixes such as a bubble baths are insufficient in the absence of sustained, incremental changes of habit that collectively make up Radical Self-Care.

Relaxation

Chatterjee (2018a) advocates for the inclusion of intentional relaxation as a component of ongoing self-care and as an enhancement to all other self-care practices. He identifies the first step of relaxation as "giving yourself permission to relax" (p. 20). The phrase sounds so obvious that you may wonder who needs permission to relax. How many educators do you know that fit any or all of the following profiles?

- They are always busy, they thrive on having lots to do, and they see it as a personal honor that they are able to multitask and accomplish so much in a short period of time.
- In addition to their teaching responsibilities, they are overloaded with responsibilities in their personal lives, are frequently in service to others, or are a caretaker of others. For this type of individual, personal relaxation means neglecting one or more of their many responsibilities.
- This is a person who is in a state of perpetual agitation, overschedules events and appointments, and is always "running somewhere."

You get the point: Some people simply have belief systems that reject the value of relaxation. These individuals have experienced the frequently culturally based and gender-specific messaging that their value is specific to how much they care for other people and how much they do.

Chatterjee states the benefits of relaxing, although challenging for some people, can contribute to improved resilience, reduced feelings of stress, a more balanced outlook, and many other health benefits. He suggests five strategies for relaxing, the first of which is an excellent starting point: Allow yourself "Me-Time" every day in the form of 15 minutes spent on something you do alone and without your digital device. (It may be difficult at first to part ways with your digital device—even for 15 minutes—but just try it.) While 15 minutes may seem like a very short period of time, like the other Radical Self-Care areas of focus, we start with one small change until it becomes habitual. Keep in mind that relaxation is a universal need—there is good reason to choose it as your primary area of focus. Chatterjee's other relaxation strategies are becoming digital device-free for a day, keeping a gratitude journal, becoming still for five minutes each day, and eating one meal a day without digital devices at a table (Chatterjee, 2018a).

Achor (2010) distinguishes between two categories of relaxation: passive and active leisure. Passive leisure, such as watching TV or scrolling on social media, might engage you for about 30 minutes, after which you are likely to experience feelings of apathy. In contrast, active leisure, which requires an initial effort, such as hobbies or games, enhances concentration, motivation, and a sense of enjoyment. Thus, the benefit of active leisure and "Me-Time" is helpful to the participant's brain health and mood. Radical Self-Care encourages 15 minutes of relaxation each day. Consider the type of relaxation you will choose to implement daily. Some suggestions are reading, singing, dancing, taking a class, cooking, gardening, and going for a walk (Chatterjee, 2018a).

Nutrition

The second intentional aspect of Radical Self-Care is nutrition. What is your daily intake of fruits and vegetables? The nutrition aspect of Radical Self-Care is based on the concept of eating the "plant-based rainbow" as a guide to eating a diversity of micronutrients, including a healthy amount of fruits and vegetables. But this isn't a "one-size-fits-all" program. Nutrition is highly personalized since there are as many different health needs as there are fruits and vegetables. Nutrition is a form of self-care that supports the brain health aspects of exercise and sleep: We need to consider how the foods and beverages we choose can contribute to our goals of consistent exercise and good sleep. Nutrition includes water, high-quality oils, and the highest-quality protein sources, either from plants and/or animals. The planet benefits when animal sources of protein are sustainable: pasture-raised, organically fed, and wild-caught. Among the great variety of eating plans and philosophies, find one that creates observable and measurable improvements in your health. Notice how you feel after you eat. What are foods that clearly do not support your long-term fitness? For example, take foods containing large amounts of refined sugars—did you know that by cutting back on your sugar consumption, you can retrain your taste buds to no longer crave these foods? Hydrogenated oils are also best to avoid, as well as any others that can be detrimental to your health. Chatterjee (2018a) advocates eating five different vegetables every day and drinking eight glasses of water per day—a change that is relatively easy to implement.

Sleep

Americans are notoriously sleep-deprived, and that condition is exacerbated by stress and poor nutrition. Sleep deprivation is harmful to brain health and compromises physical recovery from exercise or illnesses. It diminishes the body's ability to dissipate cortisol, which can harm the brain and cardiovascular, immune, and digestive systems. A frequently recommended goal is to consistently achieve seven to nine hours of sleep, per night, without interruptions. This consistent sleep pattern provides a myriad of benefits to your brain, yet many people do not achieve the ideal because they are challenged to fall asleep or remain asleep. As you work to find your perfect number of hours of uninterrupted sleep that causes you to awaken refreshed and restored, notice what interrupts your sleep and start working to minimize the disruptions.

> *Sleep is the most effective thing you can do to reset your brain and body health.*
> **—Dr. Matthew Walker**

Among many factors that prevent sleep, the most noted is the use of electronic devices just before bed or while in bed. Their screens interrupt melatonin production, the hormone that contributes to restful and sustained sleep. Interestingly, the same devices also provide resources, via apps, to mitigate stress or provide music or stories to induce sleeping. The best practice is to remove devices for one to two hours before sleep, and if beneficial, use an app that supports your sleep by placing the device as far away as possible in your sleep space, with the screen face down, and set on *do not disturb*. Also, avoid consuming alcoholic beverages close to bedtime since they can cause disruptions of sleep.

Many of my Radical Self-Care workshop participants disclosed that they started their sleep past midnight, slept five hours or less on average, or woke up and never returned to sleep. They had normalized being sleep-deprived and had accepted it as a reality they could not change. A strategy to begin to improve your sleep is to build a routine or habit that helps your body and brain prepare to sleep and begin to release melatonin, the sleep-inducing hormone. For example, prepare the room where you sleep to be dark and quiet, and set your thermostat to a temperature that supports your ability to fall asleep. If possible, address any issues of aesthetics and clutter in your sleeping space. Identify the time you need to begin relaxing to drift off based on the time you need to wake up. If you have been chronically sleep-deprived (getting fewer than 7–9 hours), build strategies to increase your total sleep by working toward 30-minute increments and progressively going to sleep 30 minutes earlier. Upon developing the habits that place you in the average range you need to sleep, you will more frequently wake up refreshed and observe greater creativity and problem-solving capacities. You will also notice an enhanced ability to manage micro-stressors (Chatterjee, 2018a) as well major stress. You will be calmer in the face of the daily challenges of teaching and demonstrate improved physical health.

Sunlight and Sleep

Amazingly, sunlight in the morning supports sleep in the evening. Huberman (2024) recommends light viewing early in the day—if possible, within 30 minutes of awaking, as the sun is rising to experience a low solar angle. He recommends looking toward but not directly into the sun for five minutes on a sunny day and 10 minutes on a cloudy day. Although the optimum experience is outside, I believe positioning yourself near a window has modest benefits. Morning exposure helps you feel more energized, improves feeling awake, and resets the circadian rhythm so that your body wants to go to sleep in 16 hours. The lights in your home can be used to modify the exposure to sunlight. If you awake before the sunrise, turn on lights to replicate the brightness of the sun until sunrise. If you are more of an evening person, the time before sunset provides similar benefits.

Nurturing Relationships

Relationships that nurture you and produce the sensation of the "bonding" or "in-love" hormone of oxytocin significantly contribute to ongoing self-care. Participating in a community of friends and family that contributes to long-term health is important for people who are serious about enacting Radical Self-Care. The impact of social distancing emphasized the importance of bonding and having oxytocin moments, if only through electronic means. Maintaining and scheduling time for nurturing relationships are critical to stress reduction and brain health.

Nurturing relationships can be with family, family of choice, and friends. And needless to say, we can certainly establish nurturing relationships with our pets. Think about the people whose eyes light up when they see you, allowing you to feel the warmth and safety of their presence. These are relationships worth investing time in and initiating if you need to expand your circle. Relaxing with nurturing relationships provides the interconnected bonus of oxytocin and the brain benefits of reduced cortisol. When you allow yourself to spend time with people about whom you care and add the bonus of movement/exercise, a shared hobby, or any activity that is calming, you will reduce your stress levels and heal your brain and body.

Purposeful Work

Working for income is many people's reality. Although the pay for educators is often not comparable with the labor, those who choose to teach frequently feel they have a moral imperative or a commitment to improving the lives of others. Some educators find their purpose through a commitment to pursuing social justice and interrupting the systems of oppression as expressed through schools. Many come to education with a sense of service or servant leadership, yet the challenges of public schools either diminish their motivation or cause them to question their ability to improve anyone through education.

Radical Self-Care calls upon educators to access their purpose to teach. Without a spiritual commitment or a purpose to teach, it may be challenging to become a Warm Demander Teacher. With that said, we shouldn't conflate a "savior" mentality with our sense of purpose. Rather, we must intentionally shift our "I can be a savior" mindset (or its equally harmful counterpart, "I'm just a teacher") to "I am purposeful." Such a shift feeds the oxytocin and the brain health that supports brain plasticity and personal growth.

Ms. Willis made her commitment to her students' academic achievement her purpose. Despite the systems that contributed to her fifth-grade students reading below grade level when they entered her class, she chose to have high expectations for students and assumed that they would grow and improve their reading abilities when they completed her class—an assumption that became a self-fulfilling prophecy. Purposeful work is supported by Warm Demander Teachers' commitment to seeing their students thrive academically. Like Ms. Willis (Ware, 2006), Warm Demander Teachers believe change and improvement are possible even when it looks impossible, yet the teachers work to achieve that high expectation. That is purposeful work.

Gratitude Is Not a Cliché

Although authors in the health and wellness genre disagree over the amount of exercise, sleep, water, or foods needed for optimum health, my review of the literature for conceptualizing Radical Self-Care uncovered no dispute on the impact and importance of writing, speaking, or thinking about what inspires a feeling of gratitude. Further, the implementation of expressing gratitude daily creates optimism, which creates resilience, which leads to thriving (Achor, 2010). Gratitude practices contribute to building optimism, which rewires the brain to search for examples of positivity in one's life. This leads to changes in our ability to problem-solve for equitable actions. It expands empathy and the ability to see the humanity of students and marginalized communities. It creates the resiliency to work to address your personal biases and become antiracist. Although the process takes time and should be done consistently, the journey itself delivers a rewarding experience. For this journey, gratitude leading to optimism and resilience supports brain health that is also supported by movement, nutrition, sleep, nurturing relationships, and purposeful work.

One of Chatterjee's (2018a) relaxation strategies is keeping a gratitude journal. Chatterjee as well as Achor (2010) both revel in the many positive impacts of discussing and writing what makes a person experience the emotion of feeling grateful. Further, Achor (2011), in this TED Talk, recommends intentionally planning time to write about three things daily for which you are grateful over the course of 21 days, a practice that I also address in my Radical Self-Care workshops. Participants who exceeded the 21-day journaling prompt and made it a daily practice noticed the benefits Achor identified such as more optimism, increased resilience, and elevated empathic capacity.

A gratitude strategy that combines the benefits of movement/exercise is a gratitude walk. Either alone or with the bonus of a friend, walking and thinking/talking about the many things that inspire gratitude can be the stress reducer that starts or ends the day. Imagine the positive hormones released from contemplating gratitude instead of reviewing and reliving frustrating conversations and interactions with members of your school community. Imagine the relaxation you will experience after a gratitude walk.

Brain Health

The strategies for changing our behaviors, biases, and lives are found in optimizing our natural brain functions and improving our brain health.

> *A healthy brain is . . . new ideas and new people. A brain [that is] less dismissive and more welcome.*
> **—Gupta (2012)**

All the strategies of Radical Self-Care work together to support a healthy brain. Movement/exercise creates new brain cells in the hippocampus, which also stores memories. When you move, you experience the release of neurochemicals of dopamine and serotonin. These chemicals increase your energy, decrease anxiety and periods of non-clinical depression, and change your mood. In her podcast interview with Chatterjee (2023), Suzuki (2017) reminds educators who desire to engage in Radical Self-Care that movement is the most important thing that you can do for your health.

The question of how much time it takes to experience these increases is frequently asked. Both Drs. Suzuki and Chatterjee (2023) in their own research and life experiences came to similar conclusions. They found that four or five minutes of exercise evidenced an increase in health. Dr. Suzuki's research (2017) shows that 10 minutes of walking improved hippocampus growth; in fact, exercise (movement) was the only action that stimulated such growth.

Achor (2010) and Suzuki (Chatterjee, 2023) encourage brain health through the creation of habits that support movement/exercise. Again, just one small action or bite-sized change will lead to habits and actions that stick. Now, combine this with gratitude and self-praise, and you are well on the path to Radical Self-Care. Just remind yourself that it all starts with taking action wherever you are on your health continuum.

Embracing self-care as a "spiritual discipline" in her book *Sacred Self-Care*, author Chanequa Walker-Barnes includes encouragement and activities to support the reader who will appreciate the inclusion of spirituality as an aspect of implementing self-care. Walker-Barnes notes that she experienced health challenges (similar to mine) that led her to "embark on a journey of self-care with a few small changes" (2023, p. 6).

Implementation of Radical Self-Care

Ms. Estrella, teacher who is in her sixth year of teaching, stated:

> Radical Self-Care is extremely important, I think, especially for teachers. I also think it is ironically one of the hardest things to do as a public-school teacher . . . there is so much to focus throughout the year on all the expectations and deadlines. But it's definitely a critical part of what general education should be trying to foster, more wellness with their teachers. It is overwhelming sometimes. There are days when people question "Do I want to be in this space anymore?"—to a point of feeling "I'm being abused at work." . . . Being able to find time to take care of ourselves definitely is the key in allowing us to be the best teachers we can be.

Reflection

Using a journal or other source to write and reflect, ask participants the following questions. In doing so, ask them to write a detailed reflection. This is not a quick exercise. Slow down and enjoy the process. If possible, facilitate pairs or small-group discussions with participants.

- What is your "why" for initiating Radical Self-Care?
- Have you experienced indicators that suggest you need Radical Self-Care—brain fog, insomnia, mismanagement of stress, tension in relationships, memory confusion, weight gain, or loss?
- Do you remember being told or hearing that self-care is selfish? What are your thoughts about self-care as selfish behavior?
- Where will you start or, more specifically, what area of your life will you address with one small change to increase your health?
- Do you need to seek professional medical attention for any aspect of your life? If so, when are you scheduling an appointment?
- What is your current health care routine?
- Do you move or exercise consistently?
- If your movement is restricted, what area of Radical Self-Care will you as an educator select?
- How would you describe your nutrition? Are you eating in ways that are healthy and not completely dependent upon highly processed, highly sweetened, and fried foods?
- How is your sleep routine? Are your bedtimes and wake-up times consistent? Do you sleep all evening? Do you feel refreshed when you wake up?
- Do you have a relationship and frequently interact with people who cause you to feel oxytocin or joy in their presence?
- Do you feel your work is purposeful? Do you volunteer or have responsibilities for which you feel a sense of purpose?

- What is the one area of your life in which you are willing to make one change and then focus on making the change for a minimum of 21 days? Schedule the action on your calendar. Identify an accountability partner who will celebrate with you every time you achieve an action.
- Add 15 minutes of relaxation every day. You do not have to be inactive to relax. Cooking, for instance, can be incorporated into this time if it calms you.
- For a minimum of 21 days, write three things for which you're grateful and why.
- How do the variables of race, socioeconomic status, and ablism impact the need and implementation of Radial Self-Care?

The Journey to Warm Demander Teaching

3

The Author Reflects

At the end of a professional development session, a teacher stated to the group and me:

> As a white male teacher, even more especially for the Black men in my classroom, . . . I strove to build a classroom that felt inclusive, that felt supportive, a place where my students would want to be—and in doing so, I think that I stopped demanding things from them.
>
> More than that, I think that I don't know how to do both: I ask them to do things, or sometimes I straight out tell them to do things . . . but to demand, for me, has seemed at odds with my desire to be a warm teacher. How do I demand things of my students, how do I push them and not go easy on them, but also show them that I care about them and that I'm here for them?
>
> I feel comfortable that I am a warm teacher—a positive presence for my students, someone who wants to make them feel welcome—but not a demanding one.

My work with his school on Radical Self-Care, which improved the teachers' and leaders' health and resulted in a significant development

(Continued)

(Continued)

of trust, led us to discussions about the impact of systemic oppression on their students and the ways it was demonstrated in their "alternative pathway" high school. Their students began receiving the message that they did not "fit" at school starting at four years old. They were not on grade level by third grade and often, eventually, disciplined out of traditional schools. They experienced racial trauma (Bryant-Davis, 2007; Menakem, 2017) and personal trauma. The students were at an alternative pathway high school with a Warm Demander School Leader. I was there challenging the teachers to think about how they could interrupt years of systemic oppression in their schools to help their BIPOC students graduate and plan for a future beyond graduation. This teacher's inquiry initiated the extended Warm Demander Teacher anti-bias training.

The opening quote from the white male teacher reflects a common challenge of implementing Warm Demander pedagogy (Ware, 2006). Many teachers, particularly those who are white (the majority of our nation's teaching force), don't have a cultural connection with their BIPOC students. Further, the absence of such cultural connections perpetuates implicit biases, which create a barrier to forming the foundational relationships of Warm Demander teaching. While BIPOC teachers tend to have a better grasp of the culturally nuanced behavior and beliefs of their BIPOC students, the premise of this chapter (and the book) is that, with sustained effort, ***all*** teachers have the capacity to identify and interrupt their biases, use their power in ways that affirm and support the identities of their students, recognize the policies and practices that oppress those students, and grow into Warm Demander Teachers.

For different reasons, BIPOC teachers may experience challenges in developing relationships with our students. The fluidity of culture, for one thing, can reduce similarity of experiences between the teacher and students. For another, the students can be influenced by prior experiences with educators who were not Warm Demander Teachers. Therefore, students' healthy response of waiting to develop the trust that supports a suitable classroom culture may require teachers to continue working and be patient.

Despite having had exposure to the vast body of literature on culturally responsive teaching (Delpit, 1995; Irvine, 1990, 2003; Irvine & Armento, 2001; Ladson-Billings, 1994), many teachers struggle to authentically become culturally responsive educators for our students. This chapter explores cultural humility (Tervalon & Murray-Garcia, 1998) as a framework for teachers to continue working to remove the cultural/racial identity barriers that impede our students' academic, socioemotional success, and leadership development.

Breathe

Before you read the next section, pause here, and take a deep breath. Really—pause your reading. First, inhale through your nose. Count 1, 2, 3, 4, 5. Hold your breath. Now, exhale through your mouth to a count of 1, 2, 3, 4, 6, 7, 8. Settle into your seat. (Hopefully, you are sitting comfortably.) Check in with your body. Do you feel tension in parts of your body right now? Make sure to take a moment to address any tension you feel. As the discussion on the issues of power, racism, and bias begins and you feel your body tense up, notice the awareness that this is an area of work. Take a moment to relax your face, your jaw, your shoulders, and to breathe. You'll be asked to pause and to check in with your body frequently throughout this chapter and to notice your somatic responses to the topics in the chapter (Menakem, 2017). This is a part of the inner work you will need to ground yourself and become open to the uncomfortable yet beneficial discussions that will take place throughout your Warm Demander Teacher transformation.

Graphic source: istock.com/Skarin

BIPOC teachers, having processed many of these somatic responses in their life, can become an ally or trusted adult for students giving them a needed respite from the emotional challenges experienced with teachers with whom they do not feel safe.

Readers are familiar with the following statistics if they have been engaged in educational and racial equity work. The numbers and percentages of white teachers occur in greater frequency than BIPOC teachers, and the number of white teachers is disproportionate to the percentages of BIPOC children in our schools.

The National Center for Education Statistics (2023) reports the following demographic percentages of public school teachers during the 2020–21 school year:

- 80% White
- 9% Hispanic
- 6% Black
- 2% Asian
- 2% Two or more races
- Less than 1% American Indian/Alaska Native
- Less than .5% Pacific Islander

However, during the same year, the percentages of K–12 students were as follows:

- 45% White
- 28% Hispanic
- 15% Black
- 5.5% Asian
- 5% Two or more races
- 0.9% American Indian/Alaska Native

Reflection

- Is it important for our students to have teachers who share their cultural/racial identity?
- What are the challenges for BIPOC teachers to develop productive relationships with students who share their cultural/racial identity?
- How can schools support students when they have teachers who do not share their cultural/racial identity?
- For teachers who do not share their students' cultural/racial identity, what can be done to improve the experiences of our students in school?

Cultural Humility

Analyzing and dismantling cultural bias for teachers is a continuous and intentional process. Research and anecdotal data from educators frequently note how teachers' biases create a barrier that prevents them from developing authentic relationships with students. All humans possess biases that can be disrupted with sustained effort. The presence of teacher biases often carries harmful consequences. For our students, such biases undercut their positive experiences with school and learning and work against attaining academic achievement. Moreover, the divisiveness of our current political climate discourages authentic self-reflection by teachers regarding biases about students who do not share the teacher's cultural and racial identities and in discussing the impact of race on academic achievement and ways to disrupt systems of oppression in schools. Teachers committed to their authentic growth ask, "What do I do now?" In fact, authentically asking that question is necessary inner work. You'll be on the best path forward to becoming a Warm Demander Teacher if you can sit with the discomfort that accompanies the awareness that you have biases, be they racial, gender, class, ability, or those that limit your skills in forming a community with people whose lives are different from yours.

Ultimately, it is on you to do the work to interrupt and disrupt your demonstration of biases. This work requires that you *willingly* engage in conversations, written reflections, and identifying behaviors that require change and then work to change to harmful behaviors. While engaging in this work, stopping to be aware of controlling your breathing, calming your mind, acknowledging discomfort, and continuing is required.

The classic work of Tervalon and Murray-Garcia (1998) on cultural humility is significant for this process, providing a more accessible framework for addressing the difficult topic of implicit bias in a challenging political climate. Since the introduction of cultural humility, the medical profession has continued to study the work, and the continued research is applicable in schools with teachers (Davis & Hook, 2019; Foronda, 2020; Gallardo, 2014; Moon & Sandage, 2019).

Davis and Hook (2019) noted that "cultural humility scholarship accelerated during heated political and religious polarization," making this theory applicable to contemporary conditions of schools. As they describe lifelong learners, they specify committing to a process of engaging with communities and perspectives that present a cultural perspective that is different than one's own. Humility, in this context, is demonstrated by one's willingness and desire to learn about different communities, free from judgment. Such an openness to learning enhances the relationships with the members of the communities.

The term *lifelong learners* is often overused in interviews, graduate school applications, or teachers' descriptions of themselves. In the context of cultural humility, lifelong learning describes a teacher's commitment to humbly engage with students while admitting they do not know about the students' lives and culture. Such teachers acknowledge that they don't know what they don't know (Singleton, 2015) about their students and position the students and families as the experts on their own cultural/racial identities. Teachers are encouraged to continually reflect on their beliefs about students and, most importantly, examine how their cultural and racial perspective has an impact on their teaching practice and, ultimately, on their students. The goal is to move to a deeper level of the intersection of identities and to gain awareness and appreciation through learning from students and community. Cultural humility fosters examining and interruption of biases (Farrelly et al., 2022).

Working to attain cultural humility is a growth opportunity for educators who desire to create engaging and effective relationships with students (Gallardo, 2014; Tervalon & Murray-Garcia, 1998). More authentic than cultural awareness, sensitivity, and competency, the theory of cultural humility is grounded in health care research. Comparably to health care, education also has the potential to create transformative and lifesaving experiences with our students. Classrooms can be places of healing (and harm), and I suggest that teachers who authentically engage in cultural humility as presented by Tervalon and Murray-Garcia will also experience transformation. Thus, the logical application of cultural humility to teaching precisely articulates the role of teachers to become Warm Demander Teachers. The following quote synthesizes Tervalon and Murray-Garcia's approach to cultural humility and its application to Warm Demander teaching:

> It is a process that requires humility as individuals continually engage in self-reflection and self-critique as lifelong learners and effective practitioners. It is a process that requires humility in how physicians [**teachers**] bring into check the power imbalances that exist in the dynamics of physician-patient [**white teacher privilege**] communication by using patient [**student**] focus interviewing [**interacting**] and care. It is a process that requires humility to develop and maintain mutually respectful and dynamic partnerships with communities [**students and families**]. (1998, p. 118; bold phrases added for emphasis and comparison)

Cultural humility addresses the power imbalance between white teachers and our students (Foronda, 2020). By using this framework, teachers begin to develop the humility that prepares them to examine the oppression of racially marginalized students and see their role in interrupting oppression. Further cultural humility is an overlooked precursor to becoming a culturally responsive teacher. BIPOC teachers may have similar lived experiences that can minimize the need for cultural humility. Yet there may be aspects of the student's lives that encourage BIPOC teachers to use cultural humility to gain more insight and compassion to enhance your relationships.

As Tervalon and Murray-Garcia (1998) identified in their research, cultural humility provides the opportunity for [physicians in their study or] teachers to humbly reject the inclination to self-proclaim their cultural expertise or cultural competency to understand that they are ***always*** learning from students and ***always*** examining their power dynamic and privilege with students and families. Cultural humility is the driving force to ***always*** encourage teachers to engage authentically with students; to unpack and develop an awareness of the humanity, brilliance, beauty, and resiliency of the culture of our students; to examine how our students see authority and leadership; and to understand how our students recognize care. With that said, engaging in conversations about power dynamics in schools and how one's own power can reinforce racial trauma takes a large degree of courage. The more educators avoid such uncomfortable topics, the less capacity they have to disrupt their biases and develop the skills to engage in Warm Demander pedagogy.

Reflective Practice Activity for Cultural Humility

Later in this chapter, you will engage in an in-depth activity to initiate the journey of recognizing your cultural/racial identity. Similar to the research of Farrelly et al. (2022), this activity and the Cultural/Racial Identity Journey engages us

> in the exploration of sociocultural issues through anti-bias and anti-racist work, [and] we empower the voices of . . . students from diverse backgrounds and experiences. In doing so, we aim to scaffold a transformative learning process in which . . . educators begin to develop their cultural humility and understand their role in engaging in social justice advocacy for . . . students. (p. 186)

To help you prepare to develop your Warm Demander Teacher beliefs, let's start with an activity that encourages you to reflect on engaging in cultural humility.

The school community where I teach can best be described as . . .	
What are the strengths of the community?	
The students who do not experience caring from teachers nor engage in high achievement that attend the school where I teach can best be described as having . . .	
What are examples of their strength and resiliency?	
How did I learn this information about the community and students?	
Did I talk with community members and students, or was I told this information?	
What can I do to learn more about the community's strengths and my students' talents?	

Complete the chart when you have time to reflect and think about the questions beyond superficial responses. Upon completion, put the responses away. Notice if you learn new ideas that change your responses. Do you seek out new answers by talking with other teachers, students, or community members? Return to the questions in a few days and think, "Are my beliefs consistent with cultural humility?"

Racialized Trauma

Acknowledging and addressing racialized trauma (Menakem, 2017) as an aspect of American schools is critical for the transformation of student and teacher relationships, learning, and school culture and climate. Menakem discusses the physical and neurological response to perceptions of racial harm and the stored trauma of all people who live in America. We all have been socialized to discount or be retraumatized by the reality of the harm that has been caused to Black, African, African American, Indigenous, Latino/a, Asian, and Pacific Islander people in the history and present day of this country. *Our students and our BIPOC teachers* hold this racialized trauma in their bodies and minds, and it is reinforced through daily occurrences in schools and in the media. To be sure, this is a conversation that is avoided daily throughout our country. We can acknowledge the avoidance of this conversation and resulting changes from this discussion are the foundation of privilege and power. Yet it is a conversation that Warm Demander Teachers, including white teachers, challenge themselves to engage in to develop cultural humility; this challenging work is the dramatic change needed for educators and students. This is a pain and trauma that can be healed with work.

Reflection

- Who holds the power in your school? Which students can successfully advocate for themselves, and which families can advocate their children?
- Which families are ignored or dismissed if they have a concern about their child?
- What social indicators of status determine the students who have the most engaging experience in school?
- When have you used your power to advocate for a student who lacked social indicators of socioeconomic status? Have you had your motivation questioned by other professionals when you've advocated for our students as a BIPOC teacher?
- As you work through these questions, breathe—and move—if possible!

Academic tracking, culturally and historically biased curriculum, school discipline policies and practices, and high-stakes testing policies act as powerful systemic barriers to student achievement and can restimulate racialized trauma. Despite the power that teachers hold in classrooms, such systemic barriers are typically out of their direct control and, consequently, are particularly daunting for teachers. However, while many teachers are unaware of how they are the intermediaries that shape the way their students encounter these structural barriers, Warm Demander Teachers recognize how their personal power can be leveraged in the best interest of their students.

Warm Demander Teachers understand that, within the realm of their classrooms, they are indeed powerful. Instead of denying their power or being complicit with structures that seek to rob them of their power, Warm Demander Teachers are committed to finding ways to use their power in service of their students and in solidarity with oppressed people. Always conscious of balancing power with students and families, Warm Demander Teachers integrate cultural humility (Gallardo, 2014; Tervalon & Murray-Garcia, 1998) and awareness of racialized trauma (Bryant-Davis, 2007; Menakem, 2017) to avoid retraumatizing and oppressing their students. They work collaboratively with students and families and constantly seek their input when trying to determine how to offset and confound systemic barriers, meet their needs, and ensure their success.

Authority, Leadership, and Power

The sense of power that BIPOC teachers demonstrate and the actual power that white teachers possess are observed in significantly different ways by students. Consider the contrast between white teachers' power and that of African American Warm Demander Teachers.

African American teachers who are Warm Demanders demonstrate a sense of authority and leadership that is grounded in an intentional, antiracist cultural/racial identity. In my research, (Ware, 2006), I analyzed what African American teachers believed about each student's ability to be successful. I found that African American Warm Demander Teachers rejected deficit discourses that communicate that our students cannot be academically successful. Further, the teachers rejected internalizing anti-Black racism in ways that would limit their beliefs in their own self-efficacy to teach in general and African American students in particular. Although the histories and lived experiences of the Black and African American community are unique to our community, our Latinx, Indigenous, and Asian and Pacific Islander communities have experienced indignities and oppression. As such, BIPOC teachers who are Warm Demanders share an insider's perspective of community oppression and demonstrate leadership and sense of authority grounded in an intentional antiracist cultural/racial identity to support all our students.

Here is how Ms. Estrella states her cultural identity:

> Chicana, I am mixed multiracial, but clearly identify with Chicano. . . . My dad's parents were both from Mexico, but I didn't learn a lot of that culture. He was raised in the 1960s and 1970s during the Chicano movement . . . where he lived at the time was racially segregated and he was not able to speak his language, so intentionally he didn't teach me Spanish but I do identify with that part of my culture.

As a Warm Demander Teacher, she stated,

> You're going to be more successful in the long term. Not only should you be able to foster those relationships, strong relationships to support your students to know them but also to hold them to an expectation that many other [teachers] probably couldn't. I know there are things I can say to a student that other teachers couldn't say . . . because I know them, and I have that relationship with them. Or even "the look," like there are things I do not have to say, like a mom . . . just give them that look and they say, "never mind."

These teachers have a love and pride in themselves, their community, their race, and their students. As such, they acted differently from other teachers. The students in their classes could viscerally feel the teachers' love and responded in kind to the loving ways in which teachers spoke of power and achievement to them. They felt the cultural connection and understood the culturally nuanced behavior of Warm Demander Teachers who had dismantled their own oppression. In other classes, the same students were frequently discouraged from believing in themselves or their ability to demonstrate genius.

The confidence that African American Warm Demander Teachers demonstrated in their classrooms—despite experiencing systemic oppression in public schools—pointed clearly to their knowledge of who was the authority figure and leader in the class. These teachers embraced their authority and were unafraid to share leadership and authority with students in the classroom. The implications from my study suggest that African American Warm Demander Teachers do not create another layer of oppression as the authority figure, but through an antiracist classroom culture, a focus on high-quality relationships, love, encouraging positive cultural/racial identity, and a building of positive classroom climates, they nonverbally communicate to students, *Relax, I'm in charge, I care for you, and I'm not here to hurt you or retraumatize you. As you grow and learn and show your brilliance, I'm going to be sure to revel in your greatness and let your class know how brilliant you are! We are going to be successful despite systems of oppression.*

For students who have been traumatized in school, the Warm Demander classroom may be shocking at first with the interconnection of

- warmth (loving, culturally nuanced, critical care) and
- demand (love that is not oppressive, conditional, or transactional, carrying mutually unwavering high expectations for students and the personal self-efficacy for the teacher to achieve student success).

In contrast to BIPOC teachers, white teachers have a different level of power in U.S. classrooms. Students may lack the academic language to analyze white teachers' power, but by late elementary school, they know to use the phrase "You're racist" when white teachers demonstrate traumatizing and oppressive power. When white teachers who have power demonstrate they are the authority figure *without an authentic relationship to disrupt the teacher's racism, power, and privilege,* for many students, it is interpreted as racialized oppression.

For students who are working to develop a cultural/racial identity that is grounded in their values and rejects internalized racism, the power dynamic of a white teacher being "demanding" *without the demonstration of Warm Demander, critical care, and authentic relationships* resonates with these students as oppression—the privilege and power inherent in being white and the domination of our students that seeks to erase or diminish students' value of their cultural/racial identity.

Teachers that do not share the same cultural/racial identity as their students can become Warm Demander Teachers if they are *willing* to disrupt their own internalized racism, examine the systems that harm students, and work to stop the marginalization of all students. This process can be transformative for their teaching practice and transformational for the students they impact every day.

Reflection

- Did you learn new information about African American and BIPOC teachers?
- Have you considered the impact of power and authority as a way to engage or exclude our students?
- Did this section of the book make you feel uncomfortable in any way?
- Were there statements particularly hard for you to digest?

If so, now might be another good time to pause, check in with your body, breathe, and sit with your discomfort for a few moments. Remember, you are encouraged to experience your feelings and address them whenever they arise and whenever you find they are creating a barrier for you to engage in this work. After a few moments have passed, please, reengage this important discussion. Reengaging means *choosing* to decenter your feelings of discomfort while intentionally *choosing* to center the oppressive experiences and feelings of our students. Once you have done this inner work with yourself, please, continue reading.

Let's examine the types of power and authority and the Warm Demander Teacher's use of power in the classroom. In my previous work (Ware, 2006), the teachers demonstrated their power in their belief in students' capacity to attain academic achievement and in the relationship that allowed them to demonstrate deep care and loving reciprocity by engaging in "fussing" behavior to encourage students to work harder and to reject their own internalized beliefs of low expectations. The teachers created trust with the students through authentic examples of care, which gave them the authority to be respected and demand more within the context of that relationship. Their shared cultural/racial identity supported the unique relationship. Teachers who do not share the cultural/racial identity with our students *can* build the relationship that allows them to warmly demand high student achievement when they can continue to engage in cultural humility and examine the potential for harm to students from unexamined power and authority. Cultural humility supports the disaggregation of bias and unexamined power and provides a lens for teachers into seeing the complexity of relationships and creating healthy engagement with students and communities.

Kempf (2022) examined the intersection of bias, power, and group status that supports power and authority within the context of relationships between students and teachers.

> People with less power in terms of gender, race, ethnicity, sexuality, income, neurotypicality, and other elements of social location may experience negative effects of unconscious bias, whereas those with more social power in these domains may be privileged by those same biases. (p. 6)

Reflective Practice Activity for Power and Authority

Let's begin by looking at your school population and demographics.

What is the teacher population (percentage) based on race?

Asian, Pacific Islander	
Black, African American	
Latinx/Hispanic	
Multiracial	
White	

What is the student population (percentage) based on race?

Asian, Pacific Islander	
Black, African American	
Latinx/Hispanic	
Multiracial	
White	

Respond to the following questions:

- Which population of students is the most socially and emotionally engaged and achieves the highest academically?
- Why is this population of students identified as successful?
- What population of students is not successful?
- Is it based on race, socioeconomic status, or other variables as identified by Kempf (2022)?
- What common characteristics do the students who are not successful share?
- How do teachers use their power and authority to create success for students who are frequently unsuccessful?
- Create a list of the use of power and authority that helps our students achieve academic success *and* encourages the students to respond with authentic appreciation.

What We Believe About Our Students Is Reflected in Our Expectations of Them

Like our unexamined biases, our beliefs about our students' abilities and capacities to learn have a profound influence on our instruction. Unseating and replacing deficit-based belief systems prepares us to cocreate with our students a powerful, assets-based counternarrative of academic and social emotional success (Ware, 2006). At the same time, as has been reiterated throughout this book, we can't disrupt our negative beliefs and biases without first coming to terms with our own racial identities, as well as examine how racism shapes the lives and culture of our students. Such "inner work" is a vital prerequisite to enacting Warm Demander Teacher strategies and pedagogies.

Despite the constant reminders to maintain high expectations for all students, if we don't believe that our students are capable of meeting the high bar we have set for them, we are unlikely to provide the kind of support they need to get there. At the intersection of a trusting relationship and academic purpose, the Warm Demander Teacher can push (demand) the student into their zone of proximal development (Vygotsky & Cole, 1978) or warmly challenge them to move out of comfortable learning into a cocreated area of high expectations. Warm Demander Teachers also have high expectations for themselves—particularly with respect to their own ability to help students experience achievement in areas where they had previously failed (Ware, 2006). As much as Warm Demander Teachers work to promote self-efficacy in their students, they must recognize how believing in their own self-efficacy will make them triumphant in guiding their students to success. I believe the teacher who says, "Those students can't learn" is really saying: "I don't believe in my students, primarily because of their race or socioeconomic status and/or my ability to teach them. Instead, I believe the racist or classist beliefs about my students, and I am limited by those beliefs."

Teachers can overcome that limitation if they are willing to work to become courageous, for which there is support throughout the book. If they are willing to interrupt the biases associated with race, ethnicity, culture, and socioeconomic status, to view all students with high regard, as intelligent beings full of potential, they can create a classroom culture that is emotionally safe and operates in the brain space of the prefrontal cortex, where learning and creativity live.

Reflection

Take another work break, breathe, and contemplate the following questions:

- Are you willing to interrupt your biases to become a Warm Demander Teacher?
- Where will you receive the support to change your beliefs about our students?
- Can you decenter your discomfort? How will you do that?
- Can you use your experiences as a BIPOC teacher to examine any biases you have and support our students?

What We Believe About Caring: Warm Demander Critical Care

While most educators agree that caring *about* or *for* our students is important, they vary in their beliefs about the kind of care that benefits our students. In my work (Ware, 2006), I've identified an ethic of caring

(Noddings, 1992) as the unique type of caring that Warm Demander Teachers demonstrate for their students. However, ***critical care*** (Rolón-Dow, 2005) better describes the commitment to students that Warm Demander Teachers must attain to be effective with those who are racially, culturally, or socioeconomically different from themselves. Rolón-Dow critiques Nodding's theory of caring as not yielding "sufficient explanatory power . . . in that it fails to take into account the historical and sociocultural contexts of student–teacher relationships." Further, Rolón-Dow includes Valenzuela's (2002) critique that for "caring theory to be beneficial to historically oppressed groups, it must include a politicized analysis of racial dynamics and the complex relationship between the school and community of students" (pp. 24–25).

I want the reader to reflect on care as more than simplistic emotions and a part of the Warm Demander Teacher framework. Consider Cammarota and Romero's (2006) ***authentic caring***, as it is contextualized within the Latina/o community and "promotes student–teacher relationships characterized by respect, admiration, and love and inspires Latinas/os to better themselves and their community" (p. 16). They explain authentic care in Critically Compassionate Intellectualism as "treating students as full and complete human beings" (p. 22). Further, Bartolomé (2008) expands our thinking on caring and describes ***authentic cariño*** as rejecting care that is oppressive, condescending, and lowering of expectations based in inherently biased beliefs that students lack the talent to achieve. Instead, the author's research with teachers in Spanish-only Head Start classroom examines care that outweighs linguistic and cultural differences and therefore can be achieved by any teacher. It is a caring that advocates for students' best interests, respects their culture that encourages student success, their language and ultimately, their humanity.

Collectively, critical care shares elements of the culturally and racially based forms of care that Latinx and African American teachers have demonstrated as Warm Demander Teachers.

This care of low expectations is limiting and reinforces the beliefs and biases that our students lack the capacity for rigorous engagement, critical analysis, academic achievement, and leadership. Warm Demander Teachers empower their students with authentic care and help students recognize their capacity that has been oppressed by educators with low expectations. Warm Demander Teachers replicate Valenzuela's (2002) description of care that enables teachers to care about students without expecting students to lose their language or culture. Further, I believe these teachers are not emotionally triggered by students who believe their ***identity*** and dignity are maintained by "acting" as if they do not care about school.

Thus, to implement the culturally responsive Warm Demander Teacher critical care that interrupts systems of oppression and motivates students to respond positively (when the teacher is demanding), by teachers who do not share culture and race with students, or a culturally based, intuitive, or spiritual connection, these teachers must do more than simply care or be nice. Passive, nice-teacher behavior rarely has the capacity to change conditions in schools. The teachers must eradicate any attempts to demonstrate care that is oppressive—that is, informed by unexamined biases and grounded in the privileged and power dynamic of race.

Notably, Warm Demander Teachers' critical care is the antithesis of what some have called the "white savior complex" among teachers who maintain their privilege *and* believe they have authentic relationships with BIPOC students. Critical care also rejects the "pobrecito" or "poor baby" stance of empathy for students that robs them of their dignity *if the phrase is used* to communicate a belief of inevitable failure. Again, cultural humility and Warm Demander critical care require a level of personal engagement and self-reflection, allowing all teachers to dismantle unquestioned beliefs about marginalized and oppressed students and liberate themselves from the oppression of perpetuating racism on students.

Reflective Practice Activity for Critical Care

I encourage you to synthesize the previously presented content of cultural humility, authority and power, and critical care. Review the chapter to create a brief but clear synopsis of what you see as the behaviors of cultural humility, authority and power, and critical care. Write your ideas in the following chart:

Cultural humility is . . .
When I demonstrate cultural humility, I will . . .
Authority and power are . . .
When I demonstrate authority and power on behalf of our students, I will . . .
Critical care is . . .
When I demonstrate critical care, I will . . .

An idea to consider as you engage in the Reflective Practice Activities that are supported by Cadray's (1999) research on reflective practice is the synergy of the process of thought and action that I firmly believe can improve your professional experience. Additionally, Zaccor (2022) encourages the reader that "one cannot become a culturally relevant teacher by adopting a specific set of practices" (p. 875). I believe it is through the unity of unpacking the layers and intricacies of beliefs, demonstrations of care, and lived experiences that we acquire the empathy to create the loving reciprocity that is foundational to the Warm Demander Teacher's success.

Interrupting Biases

We have looked at multiple angles of biases as an internal strategy for becoming a Warm Demander Teacher. As you know, deficit-based beliefs stem from our biases. Our brains are wired to identify patterns in the world around us. Biases are a form of neurological "shortcuts." We use these shortcuts to navigate our environments and inform our day-to-day actions and decisions, such as when it safe to cross the street or whether a dog is friendly or menacing. While our shortcuts can be adaptive, they can also mislead us. Teachers who have grown up sheltered from people who don't look like them or whose culture or socioeconomic status is considered deficit when compared to their own are generally conditioned to believe that white, middle-class values and ways of being are the norm. The consequence is that those who don't fit our conception of what is "normal" are somehow inferior. We may not recognize or want to acknowledge the presence of such bias within us, but it is an essential part of becoming a Warm Demander Teacher.

Interrupting bias is intentional and challenging work. I deliberately use the word "interrupting" because bias is complex, and even if we think we have "moved beyond" our biases, they can always resurface and influence how we think and act. Stop for a moment to consider its meaning. A common fear among teachers engaging in this work can be summed up as follows: I'm scared that what I do or say will be interpreted as racist, or I will finally see that it is racist, I will feel discomfort, or I will be required to give up too much.

The fear is authentic for some white teachers and is a barrier to engaging in analyzing and dismantling racism. The teacher who is willing to be vulnerable and uncomfortable enough to work toward dismantling oppressive school policies has the resiliency to become a Warm Demander Teacher. Starting with cultural humility makes this step of the journey easier.

The Warm Demander Teachers I studied spent most of their lives examining and rejecting anti-Black racism and chose a self- and community-affirming identity. This was significant to note, as these African American teachers who shared cultural experiences with their students rejected socioeconomic biases about their students. They accepted an African-centered cultural identity that reflected a sense of family and developed a community alliance to support students. This helped students become prepared to challenge their lives through academic achievement and create a positive cultural/racial identity.

How will a teacher who does not share race, ethnicity, or cultural references with students develop trust so that in the class, the student can live in the prefrontal cortex of their brain instead of constantly experiencing a hijacked amygdala (Goleman, 2011)? Think of it as an ongoing process that calls upon teachers to cultivate new ways of being and engage in new learnings. Remember Zaccor's (2022) encouragement not to expect a specific set of practices? Instead, results occur through examining their ideas through the following perspectives.

They work to develop

- Radical Self-Care;
- Cultural humility (Gallardo, 2014; Tervalon & Murray-Garcia, 1998); and
- Warm Demander critical care (Rolón-Dow, 2005).

Their actions include

- Intentionally reading and learning about our students' history and culture;
- Processing the impact of their ignorance of our students' history and culture, as well as how the education system has contributed to this ignorance;
- Processing how the demonstration of whiteness has oppressed our students (Menakem, 2017); and
- Developing the ability to have authentic, open, and trusting relationships with students.

The process—and it is work—is achievable for all teachers who do more than use the appropriate words in workshops; rather, they move beyond the performative by examining the interconnected systems in schools and the role they play in perpetuating these systems. Warm Demander teaching strategies are not about *giving up* your life experiences as you unpack bias; it's about embracing the work of racial justice and interrupting systems of oppression in the space you control—your classroom. While getting to this point takes time, it is possible, rewarding, and worth the investment you make in your own healing.

Reflection

Radical Self-Care Is a Prerequisite to Interrupting Bias

Begin by revisiting the Radical Self-Care chapter (Chapter 2), identify your individual health goals, and work on those goals for a minimum of 30 days, but don't stop there. Continue to build healthy, life-affirming habits. Radical Self-Care builds the physical and brain health that will help you to develop empathy for students and families. It also will provide you with the strength to experience the discomfort that comes with unearthing entrenched belief systems that are grounded in racism, classism, linguicism, homophobia, transphobia, ableism, and other systems of oppression. Similarly, engaging in Radical Self-Care will give you the strength and clarity of mind to call into the question the oppressive policies and practices at work in our schools—policies and practices that so many of us take for granted but ultimately harm our students as well as ourselves.

Reflective Practice Activity for Interrupting Biases, Deeper Reflection

Scrutinizing bias is emotional and frustrating for some people.

- How do you feel about this topic?
- What is the work you have done in the past to make this topic accessible for you?
- Have you supported other teachers in interrupting biases with students or families?
- What books have you read or workshops have you experienced on the topic?
- What support do you have to interrupt your biases? Are you discouraged from examining biases? Have you identified new biases during the course of reading this book or other new experiences? What are they?

When you respond to the upcoming journal prompt, write it, put it away, and revisit it later. I am encouraging this style of reflection, which is based on a model of the observation of changes when engaged in interrupting of biases presented by Project Zero (Harvard University, https://pz.harvard.edu). The activity encourages you to notice in terms of "I used to think . . . ; now I think. . . ."

Journal Prompt

- When I focus on my emotions, as I read this chapter, I felt . . .
- Using a lens of cultural humility I thought . . .
- Understanding intellectually the need to do this work, I thought . . .
- And now I think . . .

Do you have colleagues who share your desire to interrupt their biases to become Warm Demander Teachers? Meet with those teachers and discuss your ideas. Remember to breathe and exhale slowly and notice where you feel tension in your body as you discuss these topics. Also incorporate movement and relaxation to stay engaged in conversations.

Culturally-Based Nuances of Communication

Fundamentally, most people, *including* students, desire to be respected, validated, and "seen" in intrapersonal communications. The challenge in cross-cultural communications can be a lack of shared understanding of what demonstrates care, respect, and validation. Many of our students have experienced a profound sense of exclusion and a lack of caring behavior. For African American male students, the lack of cultural synchronization (Irvine, 1990) surrounding demonstrations of care and support begins as early as four years old. Many students receive explicit and implicit messages, such as being unwelcomed and excessively disciplined for "inappropriate behaviors," behaviors that, in most cases, are perfectly appropriate within their own cultural contexts. Therefore, they start to learn the hidden curriculum for students who have privilege versus their lack of privilege. As such, school can be a place of repeated trauma, which contributes to a logical lack of trust and, unfortunately, a frequent feeling of fight-or-flight and overstimulation of cortisol.

Warm Demander Teachers have an awareness of the historic oppression experienced by our most marginalized students; likewise, even if not an expert at cross-cultural communication, the teacher is willing to authentically work to create an engaging relationship with all students and make an effort to provide the critical care described earlier in this chapter to interrupt the cycle of trauma and disengagement caused by the lack of cultural synchronization.

Reflective Practice for Cultural Nuances

You have read about the power, leadership, and authority of Warm Demander Teachers. Embedded in their leadership was their communication that may have been verbal or nonverbal (think of the "teacher" look), the use of contextualized humor, or trust that occurs in relationships between BIPOC teachers and students. Cultural nuance in this case is an abbreviated form of effective communication. One example that has been identified earlier in the book is the "fussy" behavior of Warm Demander Teachers (Delpit, 2012; Ware, 2006) who can demonstrate displeasure with student behaviors, and the student responds positively to the teacher's request, maybe laughing as they change their behavior. This cultural nuance was not adequately examined in my initial research because I possessed an emic perspective during the data collection and did not notice the significance of the subtle forms of communication in a community that shared cultural/racial identity. As an insider to the community, I clearly understood the "fussy" behavior and did not think to explore the power of cultural nuances to readers who may not possess an emic perspective. However, I have learned that cultural nuance is a significant aspect of lovingly communicating the demanding part of the Warm Demander pedagogy.

To create an emic perspective for your class culture, building culturally nuanced forms of communication will enhance your ability to communicate with students, and it requires an intentional focus on the classroom culture and building trust with students. This communication technique is important, as it maintains your authority as the Warm Demander Teacher when needed and demonstrates respect for students' cultural/racial identity. It also acknowledges that you hold a position of power and authority that *could* be used to harm students, and despite that power, you *do not* demonstrate disrespect or harm for students. There can be a complexity to the dynamics of your relationship related to race or socioeconomic status. Therefore, the tools available to you may not include the same behaviors as the Warm Demander Teachers who share an emic perspective with students, but through building *trust* and a brain-healthy environment (Hammond, 2015), you will create forms of communication that will be a part of your class culture, enhance the feelings of critical care (Rolón-Dow, 2005) in your class, and create more ease during instruction. You may have experienced this with the signal you use when you want your students' attention. Cultural nuance is the communication that can make potentially challenging moments of the human interaction of teaching easily resolved by demonstrating care and ensuring that your leadership it is a form of the *demanding* aspect of teaching. The use of cultural nuance warms the demands of your expectations and leadership as a Warm Demander Teacher. Having a culturally nuanced shortcut to communicating can demonstrate care and high expectations that encourage students.

Reflective Practice Activity for Cultural Nuances

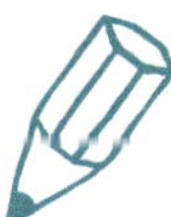

- What are the behaviors you use to effectively communicate with students?
- Are there other strategies you want to communicate with students to enhance the classroom culture?
- What is the strategy? How will it enhance communication and not appear to be demeaning or offensive to students?
- When do you need to communicate your leadership and not initiate a power struggle?
- Were there behaviors, ideas, or comments you have used in the past that were not effective? Were there any aspects of the behaviors, ideas, or comments that were viewed as offensive by students?
- Do you have students who do not understand the cultural nuances of Warm Demander Teachers?

Releasing Fear

You're now ready to venture into the most challenging part of the Warm Demander journey: releasing fear. This inner work is necessary for transformative Warm Demander teachers.

Discomfort is always a necessary part of enlightenment.

—Pearl Cleage (2009)

Letting go of fear, in this case, has two meanings: (1) giving up the fear of making a comment that is perceived as racist or makes you uncomfortable as mentioned earlier, and (2) giving up the fear of our children by rejecting old beliefs, biases, or media influences. Plan to use your favorite Radical Self-Care strategy for managing the stress that accompanies these fears.

> I have to overcome biases. I do feel certain things when a student of color is becoming confrontational with me. I have to take a breath and say to myself, OK, I'm a white dude . . . I roll through my head, What is this kid perceiving me as in this conversation?

This quote is from Mr. Rivers, a white male teacher in a high school with students who do not share his cultural/racial and socioeconomic identity. He teaches science, and he facilitates an inclusive classroom culture that supports inquiry learning and student leadership. Through his engagement in Warm Demander Teacher training and his continued personal cultural/racial identity work, he has created the ability to be in a conversation with students and fully cognizant of the racially based undertone and potential for misunderstanding in the interaction. He has taken the journey that you can take with like-minded friends and affinity groups who are committed to working through a critical examination of race. This book can guide you, too, but only you can do the journey. Importantly, do not impose upon your friends to make the journey easier, invite them to engage in the journey with you; you can always turn to the resources associated with this book and other like-minded individuals who are engaged in their work. Now, take a deep breath and continue reading.

Introduction of Anti-Black Racism

King Alfonso V of Portugal commissioned Gomes Eanes de Zurara to write the "inaugural defense of African slave-trading . . . and begin the recorded history of anti-Black racist ideas" (Kendi, 2016, p. 23). Published in 1453 for the purpose of dehumanizing and creating fear of African people, it was intended to appease the sensibilities of white colonizers and to justify the racial violence of kidnaping, rape, murder, and destruction of families and thriving communities known as the slave trade. The process was enhanced by the observable physicality and phenotypical indicators that has come to be known as race (Milner, 2023). This biological social construct is an inaccurate construction of identify or the description of any human, especially our students. The perception of race determines the privileges and treatment of humans based on America's tenacity to justifying whiteness, known as white supremacy (Singh, 2019).

Later, Thomas Jefferson (and many others) continued the documented rationale for white people to fear Africans (Kendi, 2016), which further justified enslavement, rape encouraged by economics (Roberts, 2021), the destruction of families, and the murder of people whose beauty, creativity, genus, will, and tenacity rebuked the inhumane treatment of their community. These anti-Black racist ideas persist in schools today through the demonstrated violence against Black and other students through punishment policies, dress codes, school curriculum, and instructional practices (Love, 2023; Milner, 2023; Muhammad, 2023).

The ideas also live in the anti-Black propaganda in advertising, movies, and popular culture. They are replicated in the dehumanizing actions of cultural appropriation that make BIPOC students' culture the fodder for jokes, costumes, and the names of sports teams with the rejection of an authentic understanding of why the actions or names are offensive. Americans have come to expect a cursory apology for getting caught making offensive jokes, costumes, and advertising (Gucci, H&M, and others) with an implicit understanding: the performative apology does not interrupt biases, and the action will morph into another similar action by another person, celebrity, or company. Racism, anti-Blackness, racialized trauma (Menakem, 2015), and the creation and promotion of fear are engrained in the history of this country, the soil, and the air we breathe. Now, stop and breathe to process that information.

In my experience working with groups of white and BIPOC teachers, the intentional unpacking and rejecting of those ideas can literally take their breath away as if their oxygen source has been removed. But let's put discomfort into perspective: the same vital oxygen has been taken from African American women and men throughout the history of the African Diaspora, most recently surfacing as the unfortunate and heart-wrenching cry, "I can't breathe." Take another breath and remind yourself that this work is not impossible; it has been accomplished by many educators.

Encouraged that you can do it, I challenge and require you to release the fear of saying the wrong thing but, more importantly, fears about BIPOC or the Global Majority and our students in your class. Be encouraged! Releasing such fear is not only liberating, but it is also a professional and moral responsibility for teachers who seek to be transformed and become better versions of themselves, much like Mr. Rivers.

Reflection

Before continuing to read the next section, take a moment to reflect on the following questions:

- How do my feelings of discomfort get in the way of my ability to demonstrate courage?
- How am I showing courage by continuing to press forward, read closely, and grapple with the contents of this book?
- Why is it important for teachers to be courageous in the face of conversations about race, culture, and bias?
- How can I be better at showing up for this work?
- Have I examined my own examples of shared racial or cultural identity but a lack of cultural synchronization?

The Complexity of Resistance

Consider the following statement: *"Yeah, I get it, but what about us? We experience oppression too!"*

In conversations centered on race, people from other marginalized communities will sometimes feel excluded and express anger that the conversation is not focused on them. Admittedly, we all are combinations of intersecting identities, and each of our identities that has been marginalized has its own corresponding system of oppression. Despite the presence of such intersections, the reluctance to center race in specific conversations misses the opportunity to be inclusive to and learn from the BIPOC community. And unfortunately, such unwillingness to center the conversation on people who have historically experienced systemic racism, racialized trauma, and oppression frequently translates to a lack of respect for the experiences of our students. Those who insist on creating a hierarchy of oppression and refuse to center racism will stop the conversation and prevent learning about racism and racialized trauma. While various systems of oppression may share similarities, race occupies a unique position in the history of the United States. The fact that we have avoided engaging in honest conversations about race and racism for so many years out of the fears of becoming uncomfortable only underscores the urgency to elevate such conversations. Accordingly, a desire to shift the conversation is often indicative of a lack of readiness to engage in Warm Demander Teaching as well as a lack of understanding of the lived experience of our students. In such cases, more work is needed to dismantle beliefs that are potentially rooted in anti-Blackness and are inhibiting their growth.

Next, an all-too-common statement that suggests resistance: **"I don't see color."**

Those who claim to be colorblind (Bonilla-Silva, 2022) often frame it as an enlightened position. To the contrary, such beliefs suggest an unwillingness to acknowledge their discomfort with addressing race and its child, racism (Kendi, 2016). In fact, colorblindness is a microaggression that translates to *I'm not going to consider the fact that race has had a significant impact on your life. Rather, because it's convenient for me, I'm going to ignore your lived experiences, pain, trauma, income disparity, and realistic fear of authorities.*

Cultural humility rejects the idea that you've arrived at a level of competence or proficiency. Moreover, it's problematic to evaluate yourself (or others) at specific points of a continuum of cultural awareness. The fluidity of your lived experiences and ways of interacting are more likely based on the contexts and relationships of the people with whom you are interacting. As you work through this journey, engage in conversations with people who have similar and different lived experiences and are willing to do the work to become inclusive and transformational for you and our students.

Discussions of whiteness, although intentionally uncomfortable to maintain whiteness's status quo and power, cannot be circumvented for teachers who authentically desire to engage in the work for social justice, and they are critical for our students coming from Warm Demander Teachers.

Stop and breathe, and this time and let's add visualization of your Warm Demander classroom. As you breathe, think about a class where you and your students are relaxed and experiencing an enjoyable class discussion about your curriculum and a critical examination of the curriculum and how it connects with previous and future lessons. An external observer would notice the relaxed climate (potentially with a noisy and engaging discussion) that you and your student leaders are posing and answering questions from their classmates. Students are enjoying learning. You have the freedom to clarify ideas and ask or answer questions too. Continue to breathe. The image I'm encouraging you to envision is not only possible but the result of your Radical Self-Care and intentional work understanding your cultural and racial identity.

Cultural/Racial Identity Activity Instructions

This activity can be completed individually, in pairs, and as a large-group activity. I suggest that you have water to refresh yourself and plan to take time to remember and write detailed notes. For your initial engagement, think about your students' experiences, but do not engage in questions with your students. This activity is for you to start your journey to become a Warm Demander Teacher.

Cultural/Racial Identity Journey

While doing the work, if the topics stimulate cortisol for you, implement a Radical Self-Care strategy for minimizing stress, such as deep breathing, taking a walk, or processing your thoughts with your accountability partner who is also willing to participate in your Cultural/Racial Identity Journey (see Figure 3.1). Remind yourself that this journey is not about fault or creating guilt; rather, this is to help teachers identify places in their life's journey that gave them the ideas and beliefs that are impacting their capacity for Warm Demander pedagogy.

FIGURE 3.1 Cultural/Racial Identity Journey

Childhood	Who were you told to be by your family? How did you develop this identity? Who were the family and friends who influenced this identity? What are specific stories you were told?	What are your students' experiences at their present school?
Cultural identity	Describe the cultural norms of your childhood. Were you a part of the dominant cultural identity in your neighborhood? Which holidays were celebrated? How were the holidays celebrated? How many of these celebrations had distinct messages about your identity?	What are your students' experiences that are forming their cultural identity?

Racial identity	Describe the discussions of race from your childhood. Were you a part of the dominant racial identity in your neighborhood? What were the stories or perception of your racial identity as told to you by the people in your community? What were the stories or perceptions of people who were the "other" told to you be the people in your community? What did the media tell you about the "other" people?	What are your students' experiences related to their racial identities in their school? How is selection for Gifted and Talented or Advanced Placement classes or other favorable opportunities impacted by observable race and racial ambiguity?
Experiences with schools	Describe your elementary, middle/junior, and high school experiences. What was the community's opinion of the school? Where was the school located? Describe the environment. Did you want to attend this school? Were you the dominant culture of the school? How were you treated? Did you feel valued? How were you and your friends treated by the adults at the school?	Describe your students' perspective of their school experiences. Do your students feel safe? What are the disproportionality indicators in school, such as discipline in your school? What are the indicators of equitable practices?
Who you have become	What traditions have you maintained since childhood? How do you celebrate those traditions? Describe a time when your culture was not the dominant culture in a place or event. Did it occur when you traveled? Was it related to employment or your social life? Did you assimilate into the culture? Were you expected to assimilate to the values and behaviors of the dominant culture?	Who do your students want to become? What identity are they creating? How are you helping them?

Reflection

Group or Partner Discussions to Unpack Lived Experiences

Upon completing the Cultural/Racial Identity Journey and working with trusted friends or colleagues who are willing to unpack their experiences, review and discuss your responses. Based on the group dynamics, engagement procedures may be necessary. If the group needs support in creating effective procedures, review Singleton's (2015) Four Agreements of Courageous Conversation:

- Stay engaged
- Experience discomfort
- Speak your truth
- Expect and accept nonclosure (p. 70)

Consider adding agreements that fit the comfort level of the group, especially teachers who have engaged in this work, such as this:

- Shared stories or anecdotes are open for review of biases or deficit language.

  Ask participants, "Are there biases or deficit beliefs you are ready to examine in that story?

Questions for Your Partner or Group Discussion

You and Your Students: Parallels and Divergences

- How are your lived experiences like those of your students?
- What are your own and your students' shared beliefs about personal values and family values?
- What are your own and your students' beliefs about people who are culturally/racially different from your culture/race?

To answer these questions, you will need to truly listen to your students and work to understand their beliefs. I do not suggest you ask your students these questions. Unpacking those points should not be attempted in a single day or the first week of school. Do the work in stages. Be observant of comments in class and school, listen to students.

Importantly, be gracious and caring of yourself as you do your internal work to interrupt the impact of systemic oppression in your life.

- How are your lived experiences different from your students?
- How are your beliefs about your personal value and family value different?
- What are the differences in your beliefs about people who are culturally, racially, or socioeconomically different from you and your students?

Be Observant

Notice the communication styles of students and teachers.

- What is the difference in language, tone, and inflection when students and teachers talk with people they like and trust?
- As you observe, what are the indicators of a potential lack of trust?
- Based on what you observed, do you believe that your students trust their teacher?

Finally, breathe deeply and consistently engage in your personal Radical Self-Care practices. You are examining beliefs and biases that originated in the 14th century and are a part of the fabric and soil of this country. Be gracious with yourself and remain vigilant about learning, growing, and interrupting your biases. Your students and your heart are counting on you.

The Journey Continues 4

Identity Development of Warm Demander Teachers

In the previous chapter, I asked you to consider several ideas. I asked you to embark on a journey of introspection to uncover your beliefs and biases. I asked you to think about how such deficit thinking impacts your expectations of your students. I asked you to confront the fears that surface when you begin to interrupt your biases.

Whiteness and the Emotions It Evokes

> *If you're going to hold someone down, you're going to have to hold on by the other end of the chain. You are confined by your own repression.*
>
> **—Toni Morrison (2020)**

By now, I trust you have made good progress in your journey. You have studied and begun to interrupt the biases and beliefs that stand in the way of forming authentic relationships with your students. You've reflected on your own power and considered ways that this power can be directed for the greater good of your students. You've considered how your biases and beliefs influence the expectations you set for your students. And you now understand how high expectations, working in tandem with cultural humility and critical care, will enhance your effectiveness as a Warm Demander Teacher. Perhaps, most importantly, you've begun to confront and liberate yourself from your fears of going deeper with this work. With that said, you are now prepared to confront and unpack the presence of whiteness, both in yourself—and the world around you. I imagine that the word "whiteness" may conjure up some additional trepidation for teachers of all cultural/racial identities that are reading this book. Perhaps providing you with a deeper understanding of its meaning will help put some of those fears to rest.

Let's start by defining *whiteness* as it will be used in this book. Author Richard Milner IV (2023), in his book *The Race Card*, provides an extensive discussion of whiteness and states that it is both a noun and an action verb. It is how white people use their identifiable racial category to enact actions and practices. Further, it is sustained as the status quo as it contains power, domination, and oppression. Think of school's policies and practices: Whiteness is determined to be the standard of schools, which by nature excludes or oppresses our students, even if they *try* to assimilate into the systems of whiteness as the standard. "Try" is intentional because our students can assume a different cultural identity, but race will always determine how our students will ultimately be embraced, respected, and treated in school. Moon and Sandage (2019) remind the reader that "assimilation is a form of oppression, in that authenticity is often sacrificed for the safe of one's personal and professional safety, and ultimately keeps power in the hands of the oppressor" (p. 78).

I invite all readers to further reflect on the definition of whiteness and encourage you to distance yourself from any disruptive emotional attachments to the word by considering the explanation by Milner (2023):

> Rather than white individuals feeling ostracized, unable to advance justice or outside of the collective committed to racial justice, individuals across racial and ethnic backgrounds must be in the work of racial justice and the disruption of whiteness if we have a fighting chance to create the kinds of schools where racial minoritized students are honored, validated, and valued. (p. 6)

Warm Demander Teachers in my 2006 article, and more recently, have engaged in racial justice work to remove the barrier of whiteness that prevents our students from receiving the education they deserve and to mitigate the educational debt owed to our students (Ladson-Billings, 2006). As Milner presents, I encourage all teachers to examine this barrier in the systems, policies, practices, and classrooms in order to grow. Further, I encourage all teachers to examine whiteness as it appears as classism and other ideas that lead teachers to see themselves as separate from our students.

Let's think about teachers who don't take the time to unpack whiteness in themselves and their relationships with their BIPOC colleagues, as well as how BIPOC teachers examine and experience whiteness in our schools. Everyone who does not examine our school policies, cultures, and practices and the resulting oppression of our students also does harm to themselves. Consider the following: Who has questioned policies, cultures, and practices and been ignored? Ask yourself, What is the source of my fatigue and sense of hopelessness about the ways we do not support our school community? Is it that I'm overwhelmed by fear? Is it fear of my students and their families? Fear of a system that oppresses my students as well as myself?

Consider that another source of your fatigue may be rooted in the time you spend disciplining your students. Now consider that the "behavior issues" you seek to control may be rooted in the absence of what Jacqueline Jordan Irvine (1990) identified as "cultural synchronization." Or perhaps they are byproducts of the trauma and oppression that your students have experienced. Now consider that the usual "remedies," such as placement in special ed, office referrals, and suspensions, may ultimately be feeding the playground-to-prison pipeline (Alexander, 2020; Fergus, 2017).

If you are still frightened by the idea of unpacking and examining whiteness, reflect for a moment on the theme of the oppressor and the oppressed. Think about how the positioning of whiteness as the norm has created a system of oppression. Now think about how resistance to looking beyond your own cultural/racial identity has perpetuated the oppression of your students. Consider how the system that surrounds you also oppresses *you*. Remind yourself to breathe. Remind yourself that the discomfort that you feel can ultimately give way to your personal freedom from oppression. And remind yourself that relief can be found in embracing Warm Demander Teacher pedagogy.

The journey to become a Warm Demander Teacher welcomes teachers to interrupt their personal oppression and disrupt being the oppressor, beginning with unpacking whiteness (Menakem, 2017; Singh, 2019;

Singleton, 2015). In doing so, they move beyond the presumption of colorblindness (Bonilla-Silva, 2022) and step into their authentic voice of race talk (Sue, 2015; Tatum, 2007). Taking part in this journey requires teachers to continue to examine and replace "dirty pain" (Menakem, 2017)—the unaddressed white body supremacy that Americans hold in their DNA and that justifies projecting this pain and oppression onto BIPOC students. The results are nuanced actions that created the "remedies" mentioned earlier.

In my work with white teachers, I frequently encounter resistance to the idea that their enculturation, beginning with their early childhood experiences, might pose a barrier to forming authentic relationships with their BIPOC students. In a coaching session, Mr. Rivers, a white male teacher who in a previous coaching session stated that he had no culture, shared his newly developed understanding of the work:

> When you ask white educators to examine their culture, you are asking us to put our hands in a box that we cannot see into. It's not that we are being resistant to you; it's that we have never examined culture because we have had the privilege of not examining it.

Culture is sometimes viewed as something exotic that BIPOC people have, but not white people. Again, when the dominant culture frames whiteness as the status quo, it typically remains unexamined. Cognitive dissonance results when teachers are asked to consider the influence of their family culture and the embedded messages of classism and racism that have been normalized (at least, subconsciously)—and then that takes the form of resistance. Also, the fact that some of these messages are subtle and may not outwardly suggest overt racism or classism makes it easier to deny that they exist. For example, consider your reactions to the clothing, hair styles, speech patterns, and other forms of outward expression that may differ from your own.

Despite these barriers to seeing oneself as a product of a particular culture, when asked to remember family beliefs about education, favorite holidays, specific foods for holidays, and other significant beliefs, rituals, and events, some White educators begin to acknowledge their family did, indeed, have a culture, including the ideas and beliefs they learned from their family, which also rejected or fed their implicit and explicit biases. For the white teachers who were not raised to contemplate their own culture and its influences on their judgments, decisions, and actions, they have learned the privilege and power of whiteness and how to use it.

Think of an oxygen metaphor. Imagine giving up the source of oxygen that has sustained you, your family, and friends—in fact, your whole world. Naturally, resistance would be predictable behavior. The struggle would be compounded because you were taught to resist and blame the person who was asking you to give up your oxygen mask as being divisive, racist, and attempting to harm you. White people, perhaps, will experience internal cognitive dissonance when they participate in trainings to interrupt their biases. And while there are resources available to help them in their journeys (Robin DiAngelo's *White Fragility*, 2016; Myisha T. Hill's *Heal Your Way Forward*, 2022; Resmaa Menakem's *My Grandmother's Hands*, 2017; Anneliese A. Singh's *The Racial Healing Handbook*, 2019; and Glenn Singleton's *Courageous Conversations About Race*, 2015), I've found that they still may reject the opportunity to learn. In fact, I've encountered white educators who have read DiAngelo's book and resisted the content by saying they "can't stand that book" or find it "deeply flawed."

My assessment of such internal dialogue—the rejection and resistance—is that, in addition to the reaction to having one's oxygen mask removed, it reflects a lack of awareness. More specifically, resistors can't imagine what it is like to have their existence questioned or to be challenged as a white person and, consequently, are unable to peel back the privilege of living free from racialization. Nevertheless, as difficult or as painful as these experiences may be, I have learned that working past the pain greatly enhances and supports the journey of becoming Warm Demander Teachers, and those who lean into the discomfort can grow beyond their fears.

I want you to take time to consider the lived experiences of BIPOC communities. If you can imagine their experiences with humility, compassion, empathy and not sympathy, and commit to improving yourself to improve the experiences of your students, you will have put resistance and rejection behind you and will reach a new guidepost.

While some may go as far as acknowledging an awareness of their white privilege, they may be unable to envision ways to use such privilege in the interest of their students and the greater good. Moreover, if one expresses such as an awareness but exhibits such behavior as being dismissive, disrespectful, or unwilling to listen to Black women, likely they have yet to unpack biases, potentially including *misogynoir* (Bailey, 2016), which is dislike or contempt for Black women, a form of anti-Blackness. In such instances, we must question whether the mere awareness of privilege is enough to prepare one to become a Warm Demander Teacher. In my experience, awareness is a start, but more work is required.

Along the way, I introduced Irvine's (1990) concept of *cultural synchronization,* an idea that will be explored in greater depth in this chapter. This concept is especially helpful in understanding some of the barriers that prevent white teachers from effectively communicating and forming productive relationships with their students of color. However, to fully grasp and appreciate the importance of cultural synchronization for Warm Demanders Teachers, you must continue on the journey of self-awareness you have started—particularly your understanding of your racial identity and its intersections with the other identities that form the wholeness of *you*.

Like the topics you explored in the previous chapter, identity work is not always comfortable. While feelings of discomfort are natural outcomes of the process of becoming a Warm Demander Teacher, for some individuals this work can also unearth internalized racial trauma. Remind yourself that the journey will lead you to a better version of yourself in that you will, in turn, help your students to become the best versions of themselves. Again, when you notice physical and emotional discomfort, I encourage you to continually draw upon your repertoire of Radical Self-Care practices, beginning with remembering to breathe.

Take a few deep breaths and consider the following question:

How long have I been aware that I have been holding beliefs that have prevented me from seeing the brilliance and humanity of my students?

Let me reassure you that the more you increase this awareness and come to terms with what has been holding you back from being your best, the closer you get to liberating yourself from the pain and frustration that our oppressive system has imposed upon you and your students.

Now, take one more deep breath and let's resume our journey.

Culture, Race, and Identity

When I initially researched culturally responsive teaching, I intentionally combined the words "**culture**" and "**race**." In doing so, I especially wanted to acknowledge and affirm the enduring culture of Black, African American people in America, specifically the culture of the African American teachers who were the subjects of my initial Warm Demander research (Ware, 2006). I noticed that they replicated the behaviors of some of my own teachers throughout my personal education journey. They modeled cultural/racial identity as a beautiful, enduring, and unifying force "between the people who shared an African heritage" (Irvine, 1990). I further marveled at the consistency of culturally responsive teaching behaviors of the Black, African American community cited by the scholarly literature (Anderson, 1988; Foster, 1997; Irvine, 1990, 1998, 2002; Ladson-Billings, 1994, 2021; Walker, 1995, 2018) and was pleased to see the congruence between the observations of these scholars and my own experiences. These common teaching behaviors are manifestations of Black, African American *culture* and extend across regional and socioeconomic differences. Since conducting my initial research, I have found it useful to define culture, race, and identity as distinct but related categories. "Everyone, not just members of ethnic groups, has a culture, and institutions such as schools have cultures as well" (Irvine, 2001, p. 6). Culture is the way groups of people make sense of the world, which leads to the communication of this knowledge through enculturation and socialization. It includes ceremonies, rituals, legends, language, values, beliefs, and norms.

Race, on the other hand, is a socially constructed sorting system based on physical differences that has its roots in early American history. Race has been used to justify the enslavement of Black Africans for hundreds of years and nearly a century of Jim Crow legislation, the toxic effects of which are continued to be experienced through contemporary oppressive policies by Black Americans every day. In the words of the Pulitzer Prize–winning journalist Isabel Wilkerson,

> Slavery was not merely an unfortunate thing that happened to Black people. It was an American innovation, an American institution created by and for the benefit of the elites of the dominant caste and enforced by poorer members of the dominant caste who tied their lot to the caste system rather than to their consciences. (2020)

Now take a few breaths and think about that statement.

There is no scientific basis for race, yet it is an essential component of our respective identities—perhaps the single-most important basis for how we are judged and treated by others. And while there are other socially constructed identities—for example, SES, language, and gender—because of the profound impact of race on our lived experiences, exploring our racial identities is especially important.

Reflective Practice Activity for Cultural/Racial Identity

The following chart provides definitions of culture, race, ethnicity, and identity. Review the definitions and look for others to add to the chart. Then, think about each category as it applies to you. Take notes and discuss with teachers or educators who are on this journey with you.

CULTURE	RACE AND ETHNICITY	IDENTITY
Definitions: Culture is the way groups of people make sense of the world, which leads to the communication of this knowledge through enculturation and socialization. It includes ceremonies, rituals, legends, language, values, beliefs, and norms. Everyone has a culture (Irvine, 2002).	Phenotypically and physically constructed, contextually, and geographically place-centered as it is conceptualized differently in different countries and continents. It is legally and historically constructed, and it is far more than skin color (Milner, 2023).	"I get to determine who I am" (Tervalon, YouTube). It is composed of who we are and an acceptance or rejection of what other people say we are. It is dynamic and changing and being refined as we examine the sociocultural and sociopolitical environment.

CULTURE	RACE AND ETHNICITY	IDENTITY
A surface level of culture is the way holidays are celebrated, music, dress and food (Hammond, 2015). Culture is "the way every brain makes sense of the world . . . [the] software for the brain's hardware" (Hammond, 2015, p. 22).	"Genetically bogus racial categories like 'white,' 'black,' and 'Asian' were built upon insignificant physical differences. . . . Racialized categories like 'Latino,' 'Native American,' and 'Arab' lump people together from countless regions and in some cases, people who speak totally different languages" (p. xxi, Pollock, 2008). It is unchangeable but influenced by experiences from other people and institutions. Can be impacted based on factors such as visual racial ambiguity, skin color/tone, and identifiable features such as eye and nose shape and hair texture. Ethnicity refers to people who share common ancestry and cultural practices related to a geographic region (Singh, 2019).	"Examples include racial, ethnic, cultural, gender, kinship, academic/intellectual, environmental, personal/individual, sexual, and community identities" (Muhammad, 2020, p. 67). Identity can be influenced by the development of a positive racial identity (Singh, 2019). All aspects of identity can be based on the highlighting of positive aspects of a person's identity from embracing or eliminating messages from other people regarding one's identity (Singh, 2019).

Reflections on Cultural/Racial Identity

- What is your cultural/racial identity?
    - Do you share your students' cultural/racial identity?
    - Does your shared identity enhance your instructions and class culture?

(Continued)

(Continued)

- What stories/messages were you told about your identity?
  - Who told you these stories/messages?
  - Discuss race and culture as two variables of your identity.
- Was your identity contextualized in a larger dominant culture of where you lived?
  - Were you the dominant culture?
- How have you adjusted that message to the identity you have created for your current perspective?
  - Have there been any messages that you have rejected?
- How does your cultural/racial identity benefit your students?
  - How does it benefit your classroom culture?

Reflective Practice Activity for Your Cultural/Racial Identity

Personalize the following chart with examples of each variable from your experiences. What are examples of your culture? What is your race or ethnic group? What is your current and desired future identity?

	YOUR CULTURE	YOUR RACE/ ETHNICITY	YOUR IDENTITY
Examples: Music Types of foods Clothing styles Event or clock orientation: *For example, what time do you arrive at a child's birthday party?*			

As you consider culture, what are the books, movies, plays, music, and other arts that have submersed you in a culture that may have been different from your own? Did that experience evoke an understanding and empathy for a different culture and help you understand the intricacy of culture? One example I recommend is Jason Reynolds's (2017) novel, *Long Way Down*. It is beautiful prose that presents the culture of a community and allows the reader to suspend judgment and experience cultural immersion. Living with the main character develops empathy for the community. The reader becomes more than a participant observer and shares the struggle in the rituals of the community identified as **"the rules"** (p. 31). Will, the protagonist, explains the rules to the participant reader, and we see the enculturation of the values and beliefs that make the community's cultural rituals. That intimacy allowed me to be in community with the main character, to experience his struggle with "the rules," and to disconnect from my biases about the culture and see culture through Will's eyes.

Racial Identity Development

Like race itself, racial identities aren't fixed traits, nor are we born with them. Over the years, social scientists have used developmental models to explain how racial identities evolve across one's lifespan. One of the earliest and most influential of these models was created by the influential Black psychologist, William Cross. Cross's initial conceptualization of Black identity development was called *Nigrescence* and first presented in a 1971 publication. The model was later refined and presented in an influential book titled *Shades of Black* (Cross, 1991). Janet Helms, another influential Black psychologist, created a developmental model for white identity development during the same period (Helms, 1995). These models and their research not only have had a great influence in the field of developmental psychology, but they also provide invaluable insights for K–12 practitioners.

What they have in common are the following understandings:

1. Initially, both Black people and white people have no consciousness of their race and its positioning in society.

2. An event (or series of events) forces us to become aware of race (Cross called this stage "Encounter"; Helms used "disintegration").

3. Subsequent stages of "reintegration" eventually lead to a healthy racial identity. Individuals who achieve a healthy Black racial identity are secure in their Blackness and can form healthy relationships with whites who also have healthy white identities. Those with healthy white identities are not only fully aware of their own racial positioning in society but commit to antiracism.

Since the formulation of Cross's and Helms's models, other developmental models of racial identity development have been formulated, including those for biracial identity development (Poston, 1990) and an integrated model, derived from Helms's framework, that highlights common elements in BIPOC and white identity development (the first and last stages) but differentiates the elements for the in-between stages (Hoffman & Hoffman, 2004). For purposes of this discussion, consider the following stages of positive racial identity development for BIPOC people (Singh, 2019), which is based on the Hoffman and Hoffman integrated model.

BIPOC Racial Identity Development Model

Conformity: A BIPOC person is oblivious to the existence of racism. They think white norms are good and value whiteness over the culture of their own racial group. Those at this stage of development believe white norms are to be emulated. Those who are oblivious to race feel a sense of safety and comfort.

Dissonance: One or more manifestations of racism cause BIPOC people to question, "Did that really happen? I am a good person—why was I treated that way?" They now begin to see the world through the lens of race. The associated feelings include confusion, surprise, and anger.

Immersion: BIPOC people are now aware of racial inequities in their own and others' day-to-day experiences. The presence of white people elicits distrust and a threat to one's safety. Feelings include frustration, anger, and anxiety.

Emersion: BIPOC people become engrossed in their own community due to distrust of white people and a greater need to connect with people of their own race or other BIPOC people; those at this stage avoid contact with white people when possible. Feelings include comfort and a strong sense of belonging with BIPOC people.

Internalization: BIPOC people "have positive experiences with white people who are antiracist" and "collectively working to create change . . . in positive ways" (Singh, 2019, p. 22). This stage is characterized by curiosity and a greater appreciation for nuance and complexity. The anxiety and avoidance of prior stages begin to give way to a feeling of relief.

Integrative Awareness: BIPOC people have the capacity to build communities with racially diverse people. They do not feel less than other groups; they have a clear understanding of how racism works and "value their identity as a part of the many identities they have" (Singh, 2019, p. 22). While individuals at this stage have a greater sense of clarity, confidence and motivation, at times they also experience anger, sadness, and fear.

White Racial Identity Development Model

The following model (Singh, 2019) for the formation of a positive racial identity for white people is based on Helms's (1995) research.

Conformity: White people are oblivious to race. In this stage of their identity development, they have a "colorblind" (Bonilla-Silva, 2022) view of the world with an unquestioned conformity to white norms and values. In such an oblivious state, they feel contentment and comfort.

Acceptance: White people reject the idea that racism is real. They expect BIPOC people to assimilate to white norms and "stop causing problems" (Singh, 2019, p. 19). Feelings include alarm, surprise, and anxiety.

Resistance: Thinking about racism is difficult. At this stage, white people distance themselves from the idea that racism is real. They may have experienced criticism by antiracist white allies. Feelings include anxiety and numbness.

Retreat: White people notice the world is more unfair than they thought when it comes to race, and as they explore white privilege, they may feel guilty. The guilt is often accompanied by anxiety and shame.

> **Emergence:** As white people broaden their understanding of white privilege, they move into acting against racism. Singh states that white people can "get stuck, feeling uncomfortable in moments when [they] encounter . . . white privilege and then moving on to something less awkward or painful instead of taking action against racism" (Singh, 2019, p. 20). According to Singh, "This is why to develop a positive white racial identity; [they] need to link up with other white folks exploring racism and broaden [their] communities to include people from other racial backgrounds" (p. 20). Feelings include relief, caring, and grief.

Having read these overviews of racial identity development, you may still be asking yourself, what does this have to do with teaching? McAllister's (2002) research on identity stressed the importance of teachers developing healthy cultural and racial identities. These teachers can then serve as models for students who will recognize the value of a healthy racial identity and emulate it for themselves. For marginalized students, a healthy racial identity will provide them with the strength and resilience they need to navigate the racism and discrimination they will inevitably experience. At the same time, we must not lose sight of the importance of forming a healthy *learner identity*.

López (2019), who has conducted research on the identity formation of Latino students, underscored the connection between student identity and academic achievement. Just as a teacher's beliefs about their students' ability to learn are a predictor of success, students' belief in their own capacity to succeed—that is, a healthy learner identity—is an equally important predictor of success. Warm Demander Teachers can support the formation of healthy learner identities in several different ways. Most importantly, they demonstrate their belief in their students' capacity to learn by holding high expectations; making culturally nuanced, loving, but also "fussy" demands; and helping their students overcome fears that hold them back. They are also well aware of the societal forces such as systemic racism that have prevented student learning and act to counter such forces.

From this, it stands to reason that healthy racial identity formations are important for both BIPOC and white educators who aspire to become Warm Demander Teachers. For White teachers, acquiring race consciousness is a prerequisite to learning to function as antiracist teachers. Milner (2003) notes that Helms's white identity model calls upon white people to engage in a "deep and deliberative search" (p. 207) to understand the racial background, heritage, and sources of privilege and oppression of their own and other people. The need for such deep exploration is further supported by Matias and Liou (2015) and Sue (2015), who conclude that white teachers who do not see the impact of their racial identity in the classroom culture can unwittingly create "unsafe and unwelcoming classrooms" through expressions of privilege and acts of microaggression (Utt & Tochluk, 2020, p. 128).

Reflective Practice Activity for Teacher Strengths

You are well on your way to creating your Warm Demander Teacher identity. Complete the following chart to identify the specific strengths you have as a teacher and the areas on which you need to reflect and initiate as you begin to consider how to synthesize what you've been reading about identity, Warm Demander Teachers, and a classroom culture that encourages Warm Demander pedagogy. Examples have been provided that are consistent with Warm Demander Teaching, but you are encouraged to add other examples as you synthesize what you have learned.

Warm Demander Teacher Identity

CULTURAL/ RACIAL IDENTITY	PEDAGOGY	SOCIAL JUSTICE
Reflection and action: • Examining and reflecting on Cultural/Racial Identity Journey data	• Creativity in lesson facilitation • Never give up on students in order to discover their brilliance	• Rejection of anti-Blackness, homophobia, heteronormativity, cisnormativity, ableism, and other exclusionary systems

(Continued)

(Continued)

CULTURAL/ RACIAL IDENTITY	PEDAGOGY	SOCIAL JUSTICE
• Cultural humility • Lifelong learner • Developing a positive cultural/ racial identity • Encouraging students to develop a positive cultural/racial identity through demonstration of a positive identity • Willingness to engage in personal anti-bias work **Your examples:**	• Self-efficacy and leadership of class • Planning for Culturally Responsive Inquiry lessons that include students' voice • Belief in students • Critical care • Listening to students • Learning with students • Relationship with students that support teacher pushing and students responding positively • Relaxed classroom environment while highly engaged with learning • Synergistic interaction and learning with students and between students • Delighting in student success • Understanding that high expectation for student achievement is high expectation for teacher engagement **Your examples:**	• Examine systems of schools that oppress or exclude students • Develop student leadership • Provide critique of knowledge • Encourage students to learn for the purpose of improving their community, state, and country **Your examples:**

Impact of the Examination of Cultural/Racial Identity

Earlier in this chapter, I alluded to other socially constructed identities apart from racial. ***Intersectionality***, a term that originated with the influential legal scholar Kimberlé Crenshaw (1991), examines the manner in which these identities, which include socioeconomic status and gender, intersect with one another. For example, consider the way the lived experience of a Black woman not only differs from that of her white counterpart but also from that of a Black man. When we take into account the full spectrum of intersecting identities, we gain a better understanding of overlapping aspects of social identity and how inequality functions (Cerezo et al., 2019). In a 2020 interview published in *Time* magazine, when asked to explain what intersectionality means today, nearly three decades after Crenshaw first defined the term, she responded as follows:

> These days, I start with what it's not, because there has been distortion. It's not identity politics on steroids. It is not a mechanism to turn white men into the new pariahs. It's basically a lens, a prism, for seeing the way in which various forms of inequality often operate together and exacerbate each other. We tend to talk about race inequality as separate from inequality based on gender, class, sexuality, or immigrant status. What's often missing is how some people are subject to all of these, and the experience is not just the sum of its parts.

What began as a somewhat obscure legal concept has morphed into an oft-misunderstood buzzword. Nonetheless, it has applicability across the social sciences, including education. My purpose in addressing it in the present context is to reinforce the importance of exploring the complexity of our own identities, as well as the intersecting identities of our students. In particular, a full understanding of how these identities contribute to our own (and our students') experiences of discrimination and oppression will enhance our sense of purpose as advocates of antiracism and social justice.

The following activity allows you to continue to reflect on your responses from the Cultural/Racial Identity Journey from the previous chapter and critique your experiences that have collaborated to make your identity. By analyzing your experiences, you can now place experiences that support your Warm Demander Teacher identity in a more prominent place in your life and move other experiences into the periphery as needed. Remember, identity is how you choose to see and present yourself, so it can be changed.

Reflective Practice Activity for Intersectionality of Identity Activity

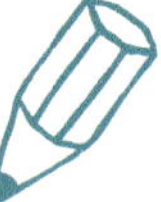

Complete the chart by writing stories or experiences that correspond to the instruction for each oval. The prompts are intended to spark memories that you have forgotten or have had a significant impact on your identity. Take all the time you need on these writing prompts and add additional pages for a more thoughtful and transformative experience. Later, after significant reflection, share your responses with a partner.

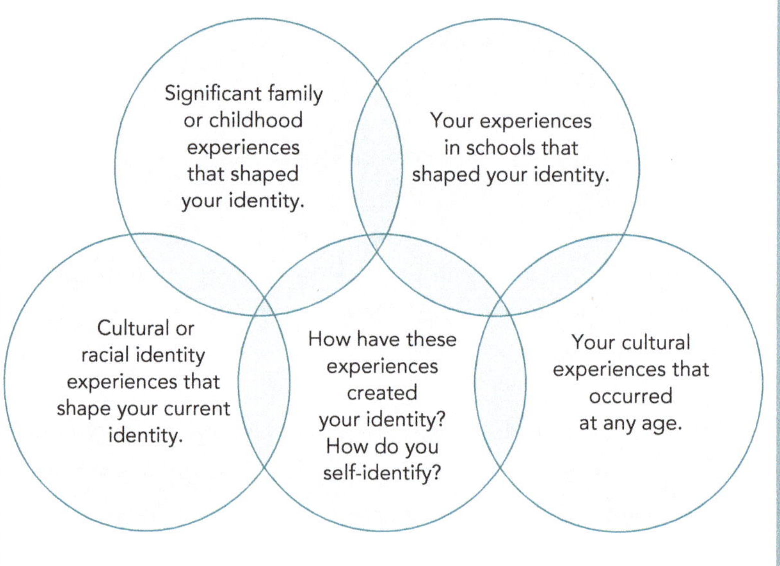

Creating the Warm Demander Teacher Identity

In its most basic sense, identity is how we present ourselves to the world. It is ultimately on us to determine whether we accept or reject how others "define" us. The Warm Demander Teacher identity is formed when we have the courage to take the journey into self-awareness, including reflecting on our own identities. In the process of learning about our (and our students') relationships with power, we become motivated to reverse the impact of racism that our students experience in schools and beyond through critical care and actively engaging in antiracist pedagogy.

How to Be an Antiracist Teacher

> First, everyday antiracism in education involves rejecting false notions of human difference and actively treating people as equally worthy, complicated, and capable. In educational settings, antiracism entails actively affirming that no racially defined group is more or less intelligent than any other. (Pollock, 2008, p. xx)

Pollock's statement that "antiracism in education involves rejecting false notions" reminds us again that race is not a biological reality but, in fact, an invented sorting system that devalues entire groups of humans and elevates others. Ibram X. Kendi, in his bestselling book *How to Be an Antiracist,* extends this definition by elaborating on what it means to "deracialize behavior":

> To be antiracist is to think nothing is behaviorally wrong or right—inferior or superior—with any of the racial groups. Whenever the antiracist sees individuals behaving positively or negatively, the antiracist sees exactly that: individuals behaving positively or negatively, not representatives of whole races. To be antiracist is to deracialize behavior, to remove the tattooed stereotype from every racialized body. Behavior is something humans do, not races do. (Kendi, quoted in Schwartz, 2018, para. 11)

The white identity development model presented earlier in this chapter highlights anxiety as a common response to one's growing awareness of race and racism. You very likely experienced moments of discomfort as you worked your way through this and the previous chapter, yet you are still reading and persevered! We cannot allow these emotional responses to internal racialized trauma (Menakem,

2017) become barriers to honoring our collective humanity and recognizing the realities of racism for our students and colleagues. I have continually reinforced the utility of Radical Self-Care in countering these emotional barriers.

Those who engage in it on a continued basis are more likely to enter into relationships with similar-minded teachers who share the desire to disrupt the policies and systems of school that have kept generations of BIPOC students from realizing their full potential. Antiracist teachers who enter into these mutually supportive relationships are better equipped to stay engaged in equity-focused work. Mr. Rivers described this progression in his identity as an antiracist teacher.

> I would say the influence of the [Warm Demander Teacher] work is I am always striving to be the best version of myself. And the people I ran into helped me with that [he names educators]. I get anxious when I think about it sometimes, and I would say then my examination of students through that context, through hearing these people who were always such fierce advocates. I don't believe I've always been an advocate, but I didn't have clarity as to what I was advocating with antiracism or my own biases. What these folks did for me was give me clarity on what I was advocating for, and then I practiced and practiced and still do every day. I am an antiracist for my students.

The effectiveness of white teachers is enhanced when they pay close attention to their own racial identity and their students' racial identities (Utt & Tochluk, 2020). Being cognizant of race has been a part of the lifelong lived experiences of Warm Demander Teachers, who make antiracism an integral part of their teaching. White teachers with unexamined racial identities and who purport to be "colorblind" are likely to lack cultural synchronization (Irvine, 1990) with their students. This incongruity not only works against forming healthy relationships with one's students but, ultimately, takes a toll on academic achievement.

Cultural Synchronization

Irvine's (1990) elegant phrase, "cultural synchronization," presented in her groundbreaking book *Black Students and School Failure*, is based on anthropological and historical research of the distinct culture and identifiable behaviors of people from Africa. Researchers who have studied strategies of Black, African American teachers identified clear communication as a significant area of strength. In many cases, the absence of cultural synchronization in behaviors, norms, and communication is visible in exchanges between teachers and students. An example, a student might misinterpret the statement "Would you like to sit down?" as vague and optional. In contrast, Warm Demander Teachers, who are attuned to cultural nuances, will make an effort to improve cultural synchronization by being more precise in their communication. They may identify the student by name, possibly adding a word or phrase of endearment, with a casual-in-tone but direct request to be seated (Hammond, 2015; Irvine & Fraser, 1998; Ware, 2006).

While in this example the use of a more direct command may be advised, additional communication nuances must also be considered. If the teacher and student don't share common racial identities and the teacher *does not have a positive relationship with the student*, using a direct statement in a perceived angry tone while delivering the command may likely do more damage than good if it is perceived to be a microaggression. The perception of a microaggression diminishes the student's belief that the teacher's behavior is critical care (Rolón-Dow, 2005), and the child notices that other students (i.e., those of different races) are not being asked to return to their seats. The student is most likely aware of disproportionalities in disciplinary practices based on race—a pattern that often starts as early as preschool. The student's quick evaluation, based on previously observed data points, further supports the student's perception that the teacher's actions are racist.

Thus, cultural synchronization between participants in a community reduces microaggressions and supports the development of a trusting relationship. Communication can be easier when people share a culture, and they understand the unstated rules and values in communication.

Despite racial differences, however, teachers can create cultural synchronization with our students, especially when they understand that effective communication is also culturally nuanced. Those who practice cultural humility and take the time to observe and reflect on the communication styles that come more naturally to teachers who share the students' cultural backgrounds are more likely to enter into positive relationships built on trust.

Carry on With Joy

As we conclude our identity journey, I want to be clear about an oft-misunderstood aspect of becoming a Warm Demander Teacher. ***All*** students, including white students, benefit from a Warm Demander Teacher's class. All students thrive in inclusive classroom cultures where culturally responsive, inquiry-based instruction, critical care, and exposure to real-life issues of social justice prepare them to navigate an increasingly complex world.

Finally, as Gholdy Muhammad (2023) reminds us, your classroom can and should be a place of joy. I witnessed this firsthand when I collected data for my initial research on Warm Demander Teachers (Ware, 2006). I saw it in the faces of students as they joyfully engaged in inquiry-based lessons. I saw it in the manner in which they participated in both their self-directed and collaborative groups activities. And while the connection between student engagement and academic achievement should be clear, as Muhammad suggests, the joy of learning is much deeper than fun and celebrations. In Muhammad's words, joy is

> also the embodiment of learning of, and practice of love of self and humanity, care for and help for humanity and the earth, joy encompasses happiness/smiles, truth, beauty, aesthetics, art, wonder personal fulfillment, and solutions to the social problems of the world. (2023, p. 70)

Muhammad's statement supports the Warm Demander Teacher who intentionally creates a broader view of joy in the classroom for the development of our students as people who see, appreciate, and work to expand humanity in our lives.

Reflection

The remaining chapters of this book explore the actions and strategies of Warm Demander Teachers. In preparation for reading the following chapters, I want to offer you a metaphor for the Radical Self-Care that will sustain you in this work—the metaphor of philanthropy, which is graphically represented by a cup overflowing.

Source: istock.com/Makitalo

Rather than see the image and think of "too many things to do," think of yourself as achieving abundance or a philanthropy of loving energy through the many actions you have taken to become ***whole and transformational***. Rather than financial resources, your philanthropy consists of creativity, energy, love, willingness to give to yourself as well as your students, and enjoying the classroom. Think of it as a gift of self-love.

Teachers today are asked to give a lot, and the demands can be overwhelming. The journey of self-discovery and transformation you have taken is also quite demanding, but I caution you to not think of your actions for your growth as just "one more thing" to add to your professional responsibilities. To the contrary, think of the work of Warm Demander Teaching as the ultimate gift, one that will make your teaching more joyful. Take another deep breath and think of the simplest and least expensive strategies for self-care that reinforce your value as a teacher. In Chapter 2, I observed that regularly expressing gratitude helps generate optimism. Since an optimistic state of mind is fundamental to Warm Demander Teaching, I suggest giving yourself a gratitude journal entry and time to relax your mind. To help you get started, I've provided a writing prompt:

> I am grateful that I (describe a Radical Self-Care action) _________. It helps me enhance my philanthropic levels of energy so that I can experience self-love, which looks like _________, and my students can experience a joyful class, which feels and looks like ____________________________________.

Classroom Culture and Culturally Responsive Inquiry

5

What is unique about a Warm Demander Teacher and their classroom?

We all believe teachers should be authentic and distinctive in their personality, pedagogy, and engagement of students. Additionally, we expect that teachers will have high expectations for our students to excel academically and, at the same time, will care for or love their students. Those common phrases are uniquely demonstrated in a Warm Demander Teacher classroom. I have found that beyond their personality differences, Warm Demander Teachers have high expectations as a ***standard***, not a catchphrase, and ***create the conditions*** for students to excel. Having high expectations and achieving them is a collaboration between the teacher and the students. Finally, they care for or love their students in ways that support their expectations.

I can identify Warm Demander Teachers when I hear them talking about their students. They may not use the word "love," but when they talk about what they expect from their students academically and behaviorally and what they do to lovingly push students out of the comfort zone of low expectations, I suspect they are Warm Demander Teachers. I can hear the mixture of frustration and love in their tone of voice, and I understand what Delpit (2012) meant when she explained the "fussy" behavior of a Warm Demander Teacher's high expectations is telling children they are too smart to demonstrate a lack of skills. Perhaps you've heard this mixture of love, belief in a student's ability, and frustration with students who have absorbed the low-expectation mindsets of educators who were not Warm Demander Teachers. You may be able to identify these teachers as well.

How do Warm Demander Teachers develop these behaviors? The teaching behaviors and ways of interacting with our students are often intuitive and culturally nuanced. Some traits are learned from observing other Warm Demander or Black teachers. Ms. Carter, in my 2006 article, discussed her mentor teacher who taught her Warm Demander teaching strategies. Sometimes it is developed from seeing what teachers have done and committing to not replicate harmful behaviors. This chapter gives you more insight into developing teaching practices that engage students academically and contribute to emotional growth.

And while the primary emphasis of the chapter is on building a Warm Demander classroom culture, we first must revisit a theme that was introduced in the previous chapters—that is, how a teacher's own cultural/racial identity impacts their beliefs in and expectations for our students. The following section reveals the experiences of Black educators—a small, frequently overlooked, but vitally important segment of our nation's teaching force. While several research studies confirm that exposure to these teachers increases the odds of success for Black students, a number of researchers are also in agreement that they have been systematically undervalued in American schools. Since these very educators are the most likely to exhibit Warm Demander Teacher traits, it seemed appropriate to share their experiences before launching into our discussion of classroom culture.

Identity Matters for Teachers

As much as we might aspire to live in a colorblind society, the fact is that we are many generations away from achieving this aspiration, if ever. Sighted people *do* see color, and perhaps nowhere is this more evident than in our schools and classrooms. The bias work with which you engaged in Chapter 3 should make evident the manner in which your cultural/racial identity impacts your relationships with and assumptions about students who don't look like you.

Black Teachers

This chapter incorporates the voices of two teachers who identify as Black. I met and interviewed them on separate occasions after hearing them discuss their respective approaches to teaching. Unknowingly, they were each describing Warm Demander Teacher traits. Ms. Lawson teaches elementary school, specifically kindergarten students, and has the nurturing and assertive personality we would expect from an elementary school teacher. She is also very confident about her cultural/racial identity and her relational and instructional skills with students. After disclosing that she had always wanted to be a teacher from the time she was a little girl, Ms. Lawson told me, "Teaching just came to me—I never felt uncomfortable in a classroom." She identified herself as

> a Black woman . . . I am just waiting for my African Ancestry review to come back, they have [my data]. I truly want to know where I come from, what tribe. . . . When I went to Zimbabwe, it was amazing . . . when I came home, I wished I knew where I came from.

Mr. Indiana is a high school teacher with a lively personality that resonates with his ninth-grade students. His father, also a teacher, often invited his students to engage in recreational activities with his family, including Mr. Indiana. For Mr. Indiana, this act of inclusiveness normalized the sense of community and relationships with teachers and students that historically occurred in the Black community. This communal care has been lost with changing social conditions, but the connection came naturally to Mr. Indiana, who says, "I saw [from my father] it was not a 7 a.m. to 3:30 p.m. job."

His identified himself as a Black male:

> I've never liked [the term] African American. I am a proud Black male, proud male. I completely respect everybody in their personal life choices.

The academic literature on culturally responsive teaching was borne out of the talents, skills, and unique teaching styles of Black teachers. One of the often underreported but consequential outcomes of the desegregation of American schools after the passage of *Brown v. Board of Education* was the dismissal and/or forced resignation of tens of thousands of credentialed and highly effective Black teachers and Black principals who had previously educated students in all-Black schools. As Black students entered previously all-white schools, the white superintendents who led these school districts were reluctant or unwilling to place Black principals and teacher leaders in positions of authority of over white teachers and students. And in many instances, the white teachers who replaced their Black counterparts were far less qualified or credentialed than their predecessors.

The conversation about the exceptional skills of Black, African American teachers may not be new, but it is frequently overlooked by white scholars and practitioners. I respect the road that has been paved for me by these visionary scholars of culturally responsive education scholars, underscoring their work is driven by my desire to stay grounded in *Sankofa—learning from the past to build the future*—in this case, the wisdom of these scholars presented in the past. In many ways, these intellectual giants were prophetic in that they recognized the forces that, to this day, continue to discourage Black, African American teachers from remaining in the profession (Duncan, 2022; Irvine, 2002; Ladson-Billings, 1994; Walker, 2018).

The need to recruit and retain Black teachers remains critical; the research identifies how their presence influences Black students' school success. Perry (2019) wrote, "Black students who have one Black teacher by third grade are 7% more likely to graduate high school and 13% more likely to enroll in college. After being taught by two Black teachers, Black students' likelihood of enrolling in college increases by 32%" (p. 5). In response to these remarkable findings, Perry made a very simple recommendation: "Hire more Black teachers." Unfortunately, the simplicity of Perry's recommendation ignores that even when we double down on recruiting and hiring Black teachers, we frequently fail in our efforts to retain them, as acknowledged by the scholarship of Bettina Love (2023).

If you find yourself leaning into your biases and concluding that somehow the educators themselves are at fault—perhaps because they are lacking "grit" or "just don't have what it takes"—consider a significant finding in the research: These teachers frequently are subjected to biases and microaggressions (Muhammad, 2020) from colleagues and administrators, often related to their pedagogy. Sadly, their experiences are much like those of their Black students. Irvine and Fraser (1998) presented such concerns regarding the potential misunderstanding of the pedagogy of Warm Demander Teachers by National Board Certification observers. I have also concluded that some observers of Warm Demander Teachers lack an understanding of the cultural nuances of how they communicate their care and high expectations and, consequently, form negative opinions of exactly the things that engage Black students and accelerate their achievement. What observers miss and fail to interpret is how these teachers do these things for their students:

- Encourage or lovingly push for students' academic and personal growth
- Demonstrate care for students that resonates as an authentic demonstration of love and belief in their abilities
- Address the impact of culture and race on students' experiences after examining their own cultural/racial identity
- Create a welcoming environment for our students

These actions create expectations for student engagement in rigorous instruction and the comfort of caring interactions. In such environments, it's not uncommon for teachers to laugh and relax with students. These culturally congruent ways of demonstrating love feel authentic to students.

While we may appreciate the need for the talent of Black, African American, and BIPOC teachers, as stated previously, these teachers are often made to feel unwelcome in some schools. Although research on Warm Demander Teachers centers around the practices of Black educators with Black students, I believe these findings apply to other teacher and student groups, including Latinx and Indigenous (Bartolomé, 2008; Lopez, 2019; Rolón-Dow, 2005; Valenzuela, 2002. Despite significant differences between these cultures, they are members of collectivist cultures and cultural norms that differ from the culture of schools.

Ms. Lawson described her evaluation experiences as a veteran, Black, and Warm Demander Teacher.

> As a Black teacher, I don't want to tell you I had to fight [about the scores on my observations]. The categories are Basic, Standard, Enhanced, and Exceptional. I got a Standard at my school. In the past, I always received Enhanced. I'm never going to get an Exceptional because they give you excuses [to not give the highest score]. I called the district office, and they sent a group of people to [explain the score]. I had DRA and Sight Word scores, all types of scores that are appropriate for five-year-olds. . . . I keep my data because I always have to prove myself. Last year was the first time out of 20 years I did not have a mentor or a coach. But it's hard. And I mentor other Black teachers and I've seen them fall by the wayside because they treat us like we don't know what we are doing. . . . I'm supposed to let them say anything they want, and I can't say anything, and I'm supposed to be quiet. That's not who I am.

Is it possible the cultural/racial identity of the observers stood in the way of their recognizing Ms. Lawson's highly effective routines and strategies that were uniquely tailored to the students in her care? Or perhaps the observation tool itself was culturally biased in a manner that failed to identify the cultural nuances of her brilliant Warm Demander teaching. Despite Ms. Lawson's documentation of her students' academic achievement and decades of teaching experience, think about why she would be rated "standard" on the observation rubric. Next, take a moment to reflect on how it feels to always have to prove yourself and to be treated like you don't know what you are doing. Is it any wonder that retention rates for Black teachers are low?

Ms. Lawson's experience demonstrates a disturbing paradox: The teachers who are needed and valued the most by their students and are (theoretically) needed by schools are not always welcomed or valued by schools. Vaidya and Battey (2022) advise us to what it takes to encourage the presence of Black teachers who are not only better for Black students but also, arguably, can benefit *all* students. And, again, these teachers are far more likely to fit the Warm Demander profile by virtue of their enculturation and lived experience.

White Teachers Can Learn to Become Warm Demanders

Since white educators represent 79% of the teaching force in the United States (National Center for Educational Statistics, 2023), the urgency for equipping these teachers with Warm Demander skills cannot be overemphasized. However, a common barrier to achieving this goal is the belief among white educators that Black students are a "problem" that can only be effectively "dealt with" by Black educators. Such deficit-laden beliefs not only amplify the already-present racialized fatigue of Black educators but also prevent their white counterparts from assuming responsibility to learn to build productive relationships with Black students. Unless we prioritize shifting the cultures of our schools and systems in a manner that affirms, values, and welcomes Black teachers, there will never be enough Black and African American teachers to bring their Warm Demander skills to educate the students who need them the most. The solution to this dilemma is twofold: (1) Enhance our efforts to train and recruit Black educators and (more importantly) create cultures that welcome and nurture them and (2) provide professional learning opportunities for white teachers with the desire to learn to become Warm Demanders. The good news is that attaining both goals is within our reach, provided that we prioritize their actualization.

Race is a significant variable in the cultural context of teaching and learning. When I asked Mr. Indiana and Ms. Lawson if white teachers can be Warm Demander Teachers with our children, both educators responded yes. Mr. Indiana stated,

> I've seen a successful white teacher with our students on my observation/coaching load. The students told me I needed to see her because she was the white equivalent of me. I met with her, and she is self-described as "white trash" from Texas. But she is real [authentic] with the kids, and she's probably the best teacher I've seen in a classroom in my entire career. She's very real and doesn't take any stuff off the kids. When I walked into the classroom, she asked a question, and every hand went up, and I was, "What is this?! All of them, eager to answer?!

Ms. Lawson speaks directly to teachers with her response:

> You have to know our culture; you have to be compassionate with our kids. You cannot say what they cannot do. . . . I can't understand why they can't treat our kids like they treat their kids. They have high expectations for their kids . . . our kids are smart . . . if you expect them to succeed, they can.

She continues by discussing labels that she has heard white teachers give to our children based on socioeconomic status ("free and reduced lunch") or biases ("her mother might be in a gang") that must be analyzed and rejected to become a Warm Demander Teacher. Again, I posit that teachers who do not share the cultural/racial identity of our students *can* achieve Warm Demander pedagogy if they are ***willing*** to engage in the process to develop their skills.

The comments from the Black educators and my experiences in professional development with BIPOC and white teachers who became Warm Demander Teachers have shifted my perspective from that of my 2006 article. The racial percentages of all teachers and students and the current climate in American schools are the encouragement to support *all* the teachers who are willing to become Warm Demander Teachers. As stated by Vaidya and Battey (2019), we need ***all*** teachers who are better for our children. The skills and talents of Warm Demander Teachers can be developed in everyday actions to create educational equity in your classroom. Of course, as a teacher, you must become deliberate in identifying the consistent actions in the classroom to create an inclusive classroom climate that contributes to high academic achievement, exceeds standards, and conveys to students that their ideas are valuable. Just as intentional actions are necessary for adopting Radical Self-Care to improve your health, you must learn and master the framework to become a Warm Demander Teacher who initiates creating healthy and antiracist (Pollock, 2008) learning communities in classrooms and schools.

Building Warm Demander Classroom Culture

Warm Demander Teachers are leaders, activists, and mentors for their students and other teachers. They also have beliefs about their students' abilities to attain academic achievement by meeting high expectations.

Unlike many teachers who profess to have high expectations for students, Warm Demander Teachers realize it is achieved through the synergy of the teacher's pedagogical skills and their relationship with the student to encourage the student to work beyond any perceived limitations. Many of our students have accepted the belief that they lack the skills to excel or have lacked opportunities to challenge their abilities. When needed, Warm Demander Teachers go beyond exhibiting simple care by providing critical care that does not separate the specific needs of the students from the sociopolitical context of schools. They examine and interrupt their own biases through reading, immersing themselves in cross-cultural experiences, or engaging in awareness-building activities such as the Cultural/Racial Identity Journey. They also continually enact cultural humility and have the desire to learn about their students while diffusing their biases. Finally, teachers who share the cultural or racial identities of their students leverage their understanding to communicate to students that they belong, they are safe, are in a welcoming "Homeplace," and that they matter (Hammond, 2015; hooks, 2001; Love, 2019; Vaidya & Battey, 2019). To achieve this, Warm Demander Teachers start with developmentally appropriate relationships that allow the teacher to be authentic. Ms. Lawson and Mr. Indiana gave examples of their presentation of authenticity, such as apologizing if necessary, showing that they feel pain or crying when appropriate, and respecting that the students are children. (The concept of Homeplace will be explored in greater depth later in this chapter.)

Additionally, like the teachers I interviewed for my 2006 article and those portrayed in Delpit's (2012) book, Ms. Lawson and Mr. Indiana created relationships with students that allowed them to be "fussy." Fussiness (as well as caring) can be expressed in different ways but should always be developmentally appropriate caring and fussy behavior. In Mr. Indiana's case, his caring was demonstrated with very direct communication. With that said, I encourage teachers to be cautious in presuming they can fuss, appear angry, or be argumentative with students with the presumption that it will demonstrate care when they lack a relationship with the students or aren't aware of cultural nuances that enable students to understand that fussing is a demonstration of care. Students who do not have experience with the culturally nuanced communication of Warm Demander Teachers may not recognize the demonstration of caring behaviors that support the demand for student achievement.

Demonstrating warm and demanding relationships, Mr. Indiana and Ms. Lawson provided examples of building age-appropriate relationships to create a safe environment. They also note that students who experience caring relationships respond by working "*for* the teacher" (Delpit, 2012) to please the teacher and enhance their relationship.

Mr. Indiana stated,

> I approach them as someone who is supposed to do dumb stuff. They are kids [ninth grade]—that is their job to literally do dumb stuff, and it is my job to correct them. Occasionally, I'll take something [a student does or says] personally, but I tell kids at the very beginning that teachers are human. I am a regular person. I don't think teachers have these magical superpowers . . . but as long as you are real [authentic] with them and they know that you love them, they will do anything for you.

Ms. Lawson said:

> They are just human beings, and they have feelings, and they get it. They understand when people are trying to help, and they understand when people are not trying to help them. I get that. I always ask my students, "How do you want to be treated?" . . . You treat people how you want to be treated, and that goes for five-year-olds as well. Just because you are the adult in charge doesn't mean it doesn't work that way. . . . If a child feels like you care, they will do anything for you.

Ms. Lawson's conclusion that, when we authentically demonstrate care for our students, "they will do anything for you" couldn't be clearer. Warm Demander Teachers build upon that premise but take care in not exploiting it. Rather, they use it in the interest of creating conditions for academic achievement, helping students work beyond their own fears or limiting beliefs about their abilities. Similarly, Warm Demander Teachers understand when it is appropriate to exert their leadership—for example, to redirect disruptive behavior or incomplete assignments.

Did you notice that Ms. Lawson demonstrates the balance between exerting her leadership while still attending to the belief that we treat others as we wish to be treated? She does not disrespect the clear power and size differential with kindergarteners. By respecting their humanity, she develops a relationship with her students that leads to creating and maintaining high expectations for individual growth.

Caring Is an Action

I often find it challenging to explain the uniquely complex form of caring that Warm Demander Teachers show their students. My goal for teachers is to commit to more than simplistic types of care or ambiguous emotions. For this reason, I introduced the concepts of an ethic of caring (Noddings, 1992), as well as critical care (Rolón-Dow, 2005) in a previous chapter. Another resource for unpacking the complexity of care is Matthews (2020), who examines caring in his study of urban mathematics teachers of Black and Latinx students. Matthews argues that the (oppressive) context in which many of our students receive education "requires a more complex view" of caring (p. 512) and underscores the distinction between "caring-for" and "caring-about." His definition of "caring-for is the active and selfless response of teachers who put students' needs before their own more" (p. 534), which is a helpful description of the care that Warm Demander Teachers demonstrate. Certainly, this degree of caring has a positive influence on students' academic performance, but it also helps them more effectively navigate the systems of education that oppress them. This is where critical caring comes in.

Warm Demander Teachers have engaged in caring for our students through a critical consciousness that acknowledges the political reality of our students' lives (Rolón-Dow, 2005). They examine the intersection of the students' and teachers' cultural/racial identities as a variable in the students' experience. Warm Demander Teachers have found balance in centering their students' and their own needs through Radical Self-Care and the selfless requirements of cultural humility. Teachers who examine their own cultural/racial identity build the capacity to see beyond a tunnel vision that casts their own life experiences as the norm. Rather than succumbing to the pretense of colorblindness, they are able to see the impact of race on their students' (and their own) lives. They care for our students through actions that are complex but also heartfelt, caring that can coexist with rigorous academic instruction. These teachers do more than care for or about our students; they ***love*** our students, and that requires a significant commitment. Love takes work, and this is especially true when you do not have the ease of shared cultural/racial identity. Rather than reinforce the biases that encourage teachers not to love our students, to quote Ms. Lawson, Warm Demander Teachers willingly "work to love students."

Building Classroom Culture

The class of a Warm Demander Teacher starts with an authentic welcome. Teachers focus on each student entering the class and are aware of the student's mood or physical behaviors. They make deliberate eye contact and offer an authentically caring welcome.

Think about the warm feelings of care you experience when you encounter friends or loved ones who are visibly glad to see you. Students of all ages notice your authentic welcome that signals your attentiveness and tells them that you are here to focus on their needs. Of course, some students may not display positive emotions when they enter your classroom, but they know when they are being welcomed, and they pick up signals when they are not—signals that ultimately can harm your relationship with them. Your eye contact (when culturally appropriate) and body language speak volumes to your students. If you look past them, you are likely to miss important cues that they need your support in managing their emotions during class.

When students arrive late, the Warm Demander Teacher acknowledges and welcomes them and catches them up on the day's lesson's process. Arriving late is not the time to engage in a power struggle with students regarding their punctuality. Let's remember, many students do not control when they arrive at school. Instead, place your efforts on creating an engaging and caring Homeplace (hooks, 2001) that will contribute to the collective success of the class.

Ms. Estrella described the culture of a Warm Demander Teacher's classroom as "safe, fun, supportive. A place that people just want to be. I know a lot of students who come to [our school] that I've never had in class before, but many of them find their way into my classroom or just come by to say hi."

Homeplace

hooks (2001) defined *Homeplace* as a place, an environment where we can know we are safe, at home, and to recover our wholeness. Vaidya and Battey (2022) contextualized homeplace as a classroom culture for Black students where their dignity could be restored and be a safe place to be encouraged to learn, "where one is humanized in resistance to broader contexts of power, as a 'haven,' free from negative dominant discourses" (p. 218). Warm Demander Teachers create a Homeplace for students in which they can recover from years of feeling unwelcome in schools. Such spaces are aesthetically pleasing and relaxing. In short, Homeplaces are ideal sites for affirming students' identities but also for challenging them academically.

Warm Demander Teachers are able to maintain just the right balance between fun and academic work. Ms. Lawson reflected on her similarity with the teachers in my 2006 article:

> I play music while my students are working . . . I give them passion . . . I let kids be kids, and if it's time to stop doing some work and do a dance . . . or dance with our drums, that's what we are going to do . . . and then they get back to work.

Mr. Indiana discussed the aesthetics of his room: The paintings on the wall, the household decorations, his tarantulas, and the soft lighting combine to form a relaxing environment. Laughing, he said that, based on his appearance and affect (a physically fit Black man with tattoos and an edgy personality), outsiders to his classroom might be surprised to see such an impeccably clean room. What is most important is that his students see it as a welcoming place to relax and learn. Such a setting increases their motivation to meet Mr. Indiana's high academic expectations.

> I want it to be comfortable. If I'm sitting in here all day, I want it to smell good. I want a nice vibe, I want music playing, I want all the things that contribute to my own personal peace of mind, which transfers to them because whatever energy I'm giving off they are getting. If I'm calm, they are calm. I have light jazz playing; I have a fake fireplace for the winter. There is room for fun, but they must unlock the fun.

He explained unlocking the fun occurs when they excel academically. For example, Mr. Indiana has a popcorn machine in the classroom, and his students understand that its use is connected to their academic engagement throughout the day. In other words, they are in control of whether it's turned on or off, depending upon their level(s) of engagement. Much in the way that Mrs. Lawson "lets kids be kids" by allowing them to have fun through dance and drumming, Mr. Indiana uses humor effectively. In this room, the students feel free to laugh. At the same time, Mr. Indiana also employs humor in his direct conversations with students to push them to work harder. In addition to class time, he stated that if they need a personal conversation with him, he arranges that time.

> They are going to get exactly what they need at that moment—if it's a hug, come and get a hug; if you need to be told that was stupid, I'll say that was stupid, right? It's weird the stuff they feel comfortable coming to talk about because they need someone to talk to them . . . they want an adult to listen.

The room aesthetics and the relational care/love are how Mr. Indiana creates his students' Homeplace (hooks, 2001; Vaidya & Battey, 2022).

Vaidya and Battey (2022), whose work was cited earlier in this chapter, researched Black teachers who taught mathematics to Black students and examined how they facilitated academic success. Their research determined that Homeplaces made an important contribution to student well-being and achievement. More specifically, when teachers provide a place for students to feel safe and comfortable, they are more likely to challenge themselves in mathematics and reject any ideas that they lack the ability to do so. If this feels familiar to you, there is a reason. Vaidya and Battey's conclusion that the combination of comfort, care, and praise that demonstrates a belief in students' skills and ability to collaborate are all reminiscent of the actions of Warm Demander Teachers.

Engaging Academic Rigor

Warm Demander Teachers plan lessons for student engagement. With time, students can begin taking leadership to cofacilitate these lessons.

Teachers invest in building the culture daily, despite the challenges that may occur. Don't let these challenges discourage you. Once you have *developed* productive relationships with the students (and you may not be successful on your first attempts), they *will* participate in lessons in which they actively discuss and engage with the content. As your relationships progress, your capacity to manage unpredictable student responses will expand.

Think about your students' demonstration of engagement and enjoyment. Notice when they are having fun. Do they act like they are at a noisy sporting event or a place where they cannot talk? Are there multiple voices, laughing, and playful disagreement? How can you create that engagement for lessons and build in learning, student leadership, and student voice? How can you achieve that level of playful engagement and maintain your leadership to manage disruption or harm to students?

You plan for this level of engagement by building upon and developing your instinct for relationships with students. As Mr. Indiana and Ms. Lawson insist, it must be authentic; students must trust you to teach lessons that are valuable and build skills students will use. You should want to have fun, and you invite them to have fun.

> If it's boring to me, it'd going to be extremely boring to them. . . . I tell them, "Look, today we will have a good time, we will have fun. So if you decide not to participate, you're not going to have fun, then that's on you. But when I was planning the lesson, to me it was as much fun as you are going to have in a language arts class today!"

Mr. Indiana uses humor to introduce the lesson, along with demonstrating an appreciation for it. He also uses humor with students when they give answers that he deems as beneath their ability level. With that said, I want to offer an important qualifier: The students do not see his response to their answer as an attack or shaming. He is never mean-spirited but sometimes age-appropriately sarcastic. Therefore, students understand his playful response to a wrong answer is not intended to hurt the student. He reflected that he thought students liked him for his humor but found out they believed he loved them through his demonstration of love. The students' evidence of his love takes many forms: providing snacks when they were hungry, listening without disruption when they needed him, remembering details from stories they told him, and recalling those details in later conversations. He also recognizes when it is appropriate to talk privately with students about their behavior and is available when they contact him, even during the summer. Sometimes students would text him—not to receive a response, but to let him know how they are doing. He shows his students these layers of love with his genuine humor and authentic "edgy" personality.

Ask yourself the following: How will you model an inclusive classroom culture where students of all identities, especially members of marginalized communities, are respected both in conversations and behaviors? Do your students know you expect everyone to be respected in the class? Do they observe the manner in which you demonstrate respect for students of all identities, including those who may challenge your own beliefs or values? Warm Demander Teachers go out of their way to be inclusive of *all* students, including those students who have been labeled as "difficult." Remind yourself that frequently these are the children that most need to feel included. And remember that you can also incorporate books and materials into your lessons that not only mirror your students' racial and cultural identities but also provide models of inclusivity, belonging, and cultural humility.

Student Leadership

Our students have a myriad of experiences in schools and the media that devalue their voices and lived experiences. Many of our students began learning as early as preschool that their voices were "too loud," that their answers were "wrong," and that they talked "too much." Throughout the subsequent years of their formal education, they suffered multiple attempts to silence their voices' energy, diminish their ideas, devalue their cultures, and control their bodies. As much as we tout the value of student agency and leadership, the onslaught of these assaults works against their actualization. Warm Demander Teachers can counter the harmful effects of such degradation by communicating their belief in their students' potential for brilliance. Rather than silencing, they provide encouragement when needed, support students as they refine their ideas, and create a classroom culture that values student voice and class.

I cannot overemphasize the power of a classroom in which a teacher will actively encourage students to lead in academics, make them feel valued, and communicate that their ideas and questions have learning value not only for themselves but for the rest of class. Warm Demander Teachers have the potential to reverse past harms that have contributed to what author Christoper Emdin (2016), who wrote the book *For White Folks Who Teach in the Hood*, calls a "distortion of the student's self-image."

Emdin (2016) encourages the transformative power of student leadership through the engagement of students as co-teachers. He describes an aspect of reality pedagogy as engaging students as co-teachers to give everyone an opportunity to bring their perspective through teaching and learning. Emden continues that co-teaching acknowledges that teachers cannot meet all the needs of students, and when students are engaged in the transfer of roles and they teach, then they demonstrate what good teaching is for them. Further, this is an inclusive action as everyone in the classroom can participate. Consider the level of understanding students achieve when they are active participants in transmission of content and not passive observers.

Our students *are* brilliant and possess untapped leadership. When we affirm their unique abilities to build and present original ideas, their creative uses of language, their artistry, and the manner in which they engage with their peers, we generate the kind of engagement that is missing in so many classrooms. When we practice cultural humility and interrogate our own biases and fears that have prevented us from relinquishing control and free our students to talk, ask questions, and lead, we too are liberated. We reject the oppressive systems of schools that have reinforced the perception that the voices of students need to be silenced when, in fact, unleashing those voices can be the key to rigorous academic engagement.

Joy

Muhammad (2023) describes joy in schools as a pursuit in the HILL (Histories, Identities, Literacies, Liberation) framework. She describes joy as not just fun and celebratory, but "the embodiment of, learning of, and practice of love of self and humanity, and care for and help for humanity" (p. 70). Learning from Muhammad's work, I propose that a basic measure of classroom engagement would be the joy students feel when they are valued and heard. This joy is shared by students and teachers alike—a joy for learning from each other. Ms. Lawson expressed joy in observing her students support each other and take the lead as she moved into the role of facilitator. In their research on math teachers, Vaidya and Battey (2022) provide examples of teachers vocally affirming students as they demonstrated their skills in math and supported their classmates. These teachers were confident in encouraging their students to receive support from their peers in completing assignments. Emdin (2016) recommends considering students as experts and creating lessons with students. The opportunities to engage students with the development of critical analysis of content and how to explain it only occur with teachers who believe in their students' talents and ability to understand and teach challenging content. The teacher is the content expert, and the students can articulate their ideas to their peers. Imagine a class that values students' identities, voices, and ideas. Think about how your students would respond. Would this basic respect for their humanity nurture a generation of students who seek to solve the problems of their class, school, and the world?

Cultural Humility

We return to the concept of cultural humility as a critical element for building a Warm Demander Teacher classroom culture. Try to envision an effective and student-centered culture. Is it possible to promote such student-centered cultures while still retaining one's position as an authority figure? It requires some balance, and it is the quintessential essence of Warm Demander Teachers. The Black and Chicana Warm Demander Teachers who participated in my interviews were comfortable and confident in their stance as authority figures; they could balance this with demonstrating their care and love for students. The white male teacher who I spoke with engaged in cultural humility by understanding that his authority had to be balanced with the students' perception of white male teachers and their potential to use their power to harm students. (Recall my cautionary note that one must understand the relationship and the cultural/racial context before engaging in fussy behavior?) He also acknowledged the fears he had been taught about teaching Black male students.

When Warm Demander Teachers and their students share cultural/racial identities, the teachers are better able to minimize the harm of historic racial oppression from authority figures because they have endured similar lived experiences of oppression and have worked to create their own cultural/racial identities. They appreciate the significance of their teaching as an act of resistance to racial oppression. Their own identity work is a form of liberation for themselves and their students. When teachers have engaged in the work of examining their own cultural/racial identities within the context of the dominance of power in America, their beliefs, and values of who they are liberate them from oppressive beliefs about their identity. Their freedom allows them to serve as powerful models for their students to observe, embrace, and be empowered to develop their identities. For those aspiring Warm Demander Teachers who don't share the racial/ethnic identities of their students, cultural humility is not only the way to understanding their students' histories and lived experiences but also understanding how to exert their power in a manner that serves the good of those students. Using cultural humility as a framework, teachers will recognize and challenge power imbalances and develop respectful partnerships with students (Gallardo, 2014; Tervalon & Murray-Garcia, 1998).

But let's not limit ourselves to the students who are culturally and racially different. Race may have its unique position in our society, but we would be remiss to not acknowledge other marginalized student groups, including those who are neurodivergent and differently abled or those who are members of the LGBTQIA+ community. An important question to consider is whether you, as the authority figure in the class, encourage a classroom culture that welcomes the identities of some but not all students. In a Warm Demander class, the teacher uses cultural humility to examine a spectrum of personal biases, including ableism, heteronormativity, and cisnormativity and will willingly work to create an authentic culture that respects the humanity (Muhammad, 2020) of all students and affirms their sense of belongingness. In such cultures, students also learn how to enact cultural humility in the interest of better understanding those who are different from them and playing a role in sustaining inclusivity.

Davis and Hook (2019) have written extensively on cultural humility and propose that it requires us to rise beyond self-interest and in-group favoritism and not use our classroom culture as a tool of coercion and compliance. The Warm Demander Teacher must critically analyze if a classroom culture creates academic success, warmth, critical care and love, and provides an inclusive place for all students, particularly for students from marginalized identities. For example, a cultural norm in such classrooms is rejecting inappropriate language that may be found in popular media, such as song lyrics that degrade and diminish our students' identities. Remind yourself that a beloved community or Homeplace (hooks, 2001; Vaidya & Battey, 2022) welcomes and affirms ***all*** students.

Culturally Responsive Inquiry

I want to be clear about the positioning of the strategies described in this section. More specifically, before enacting culturally responsive inquiry, the following conditions must be in place:

1. Teachers have sufficiently demonstrated that they care for and love their students.
2. Teachers are so confident and comfortable in their leadership that they willingly share leadership with students and encourage students to develop their own leadership talents.
3. The classroom has been transformed into a welcoming and safe Homeplace in which student voice is encouraged and honored.
4. Teachers share the cognitive load of instruction with students and believe that they too have the capacity to explain and teach content in a manner that will be understood by their peers.
5. The warmth of the classroom encourages students to demonstrate their leadership and "recover their wholeness" from classes and systems that have devalued them.

My 2008 article identifies culturally responsive constructivism as a proactive solution to raising achievement. I have since replaced the term *culturally responsive constructivism* with *culturally responsive inquiry*, which more explicitly describes the processes and actions in which both teachers and students engage. Constructivism refers to the body of theory that facilitates these processes and actions. Constructivist learning theorists center the student in the development of learning through a synthesis of prior knowledge and experiences. The central premise of constructivism is that we construct new knowledge by building on our existing knowledge or schema, which includes our lived experiences. As you might expect from previous discussions in this book, familiarity with students' lived experience is especially important to teachers whose own lived experiences and cultures are quite different from those of their students. Another distinction of constructivist theory is that learning is both active and social. It is the antithesis of instruction that does not engage student voice, does not ask questions, and discourages students from questioning what they are learning or engaging critical thinking. In culturally responsive inquiry, the teacher serves as the facilitator and encourages inquiry from the learners (Ariati et al., 2023; Hinton & Cook, 2021). Perhaps at a slower pace but more engaging than direct instruction, inquiry is dependent upon the belief that the learner has life experiences and prior knowledge that can contribute to the learning of the other students who function as valuable members of a learning community, and collectively, students learn to become independent thinkers.

Culturally responsive inquiry is not focused on students who are passively told what to think or where to find the answer on the page. It moves students beyond superficial thinking about any topic and encourages critical analysis and research in the collection of new thoughts and ideas of other authors. It challenges students to examine topics from multiple perspectives and to analyze the beliefs and the historical context in which the author's ideas were created. Culturally responsive/sustaining teaching strategies make lessons engaging and meaningful to our students. Moreover, these learner-centered strategies can be enacted at any grade level, as this kindergarten example from Ms. Lawson demonstrates:

> But this year was really different than most years. Because I know education has changed, so I had to change. So I became the facilitator of my classroom, which was so cool because I got to see students actually helping each other, explaining to each other, "This is what we're doing." We did a math project . . . and the kids could choose what problem they would do. . . . There were little girls helping one of my little boys and she said, "Okay, now think about it." . . . And I was like, "Wow!" This really does work when you let them go to understand how the lesson should work.

Ms. Lawson has told her students that no question is off-limits. Consistent with inquiry learning, students can drive the instructional content with their questions and desire to learn more, and this frequently leads to exceeding external content standards.

> One day we were talking about penguins, and they asked me, and I said, "I don't know. Together we will find out." And we did a whole lesson on penguins, and they were so excited . . . they wanted to know everything. Once they find out that I want to know what they want to know, it just opens everything. . . . I have such high expectations because just knowing your letters and sounds, that's not enough. How about we learn how to read, how about we write a story on our own . . . [the teacher observation tool] says you're supposed to teach the standards. . . . I teach the standard and I teach more.

Culturally responsive inquiry builds on and encompasses all the foundational elements of a Warm Demander Teacher. It encourages the examination and positive inclusion of the students' cultural/racial identity as this pedagogy disputes the deficit beliefs about our students. It also presumes that students have the skills and ability to engage in rigorous, inquiry-based learning where they must work as collaborators with their classmates. In the process of learning, there may be moments of frustration with new ideas or the presence of ambiguity. In some instances, the lesson might even stall, in which case, rather than taking over the lesson, the teacher exerts leadership in a manner that encourages students to stay engaged. A natural expansion of culturally responsive inquiry work is criticality, "the ability to read print and nonprint text with a lens of understanding how power, oppression, and privilege are present. This requires humans to think outside of themselves, including the cultural identities and values they have come to know" (Muhammad, 2018, p. 139). Further, criticality is a step toward social transformation by honoring the students' ability to make sense of the world through an interrogation of injustice characterized by their ability to see and name the realities they experience and to develop the agency to work toward a better world for all.

As long as oppression is present in the world, students need a pedagogy that nurtures criticality.
—G. Muhammad (2020)

As constructivism supports critical thinking, culturally responsive inquiry supports criticality. In the classroom dynamics of cultural humility and cultural/racial identity, the obvious growth would be rich dialogues and understanding of oppression for the purpose of teaching students to create relationships that identify and reject oppression. Consistent with Irvine and Armento (2001), Ladson-Billings (1994), and Walker's (2018) determination for culturally responsive education, we educate students for the purpose of making their world better.

Trust is a critical component of culturally responsive inquiry. Students who have not experienced this type of teaching and are more accustomed to direct instruction may begin to doubt their own abilities and fear academic failure. To ease the transition into culturally responsive inquiry, teachers can model the styles of questioning, presenting, and engaging in interactive learning experiences that students will be expected to demonstrate when they co-teach. As the students actively engage in constructing their own learning, the teacher is rarely "teaching," at least in the traditional sense. Trust for the teacher and the students is developed through activities intentionally working to create a family-like community and demonstrating a belief in the students' ability to think critically and creatively. Of course, learning is not always a linear progression, and there may be times when the teacher needs to claim their authority and clarify the content. Nonetheless, whenever possible, Warm Demander Teachers encourage students to be brave with their ideas.

Reflection

- If your class was observed by someone who did not know you or your students, what would they notice?
- How would they see evidence of not just an attractive room, but a Homespace?
    - What can you change to make it a Homespace?
- Is it the way the room is decorated or observable interactions between the students and you that make it a Homespace?
- During lessons, what are the indicators of inquiry-based learning?

Healing Our Students, Healing Ourselves

6

By now, it should be abundantly clear that becoming a Warm Demander Teacher involves a journey to enhanced self-awareness and positive culture and race consciousness. While the journey can be circuitous and emotionally taxing, it is also a path to your own healing and your liberation as a teacher and human being. This chapter examines teaching as an act of healing, which leads to wholeness and transformation. You are now aware that our students deserve better than the hurt that they have suffered at the hands of our education system. How often has culture, race, and socioeconomic status been used to justify denying marginalized learners the education they deserve? The passage of *Brown v. Board of Education* took place 70 years ago, yet disproportionalitics have endured in numerous school policies and practices, from disciplinary actions and suspensions to overrepresentation of students of color in special education to underrepresentation of these students in gifted and talented and AP programs (Fergus, 2017). Our students continue to be harmed by narratives of predictable failure, misguided school reform efforts that were never designed to amplify the strengths of our students, and structural inequities that have been entrenched in our society for generations. Let's remember Black teachers *and* our students were negatively impacted. But I believe we can heal.

A central premise of this chapter is that, by increasing their self-awareness, culture and race consciousness, and understanding of where inequities live, teachers of all races can develop the capacity to promote healing for both their students and themselves. But self-awareness is merely the beginning of the journey. It must be channeled into action, beginning with developing the mindsets and skills to authentically make our students the focus of learning, to leverage their inner brilliance—brilliance that is all too often overshadowed by our oppressive systems. By recognizing and acknowledging the genius of our historically underserved students, we can help them form positive learner identities.

I am not offering you a bag of tricks to accomplish all this. There are no silver bullets or dazzling technology, no quick fixes, or tantalizing recipes to develop Warm Demander Teacher relationships. I'm not alone in taking this position. Irvine often stated that being culturally responsive was not a "bag of tricks," and Hammond (2015) has reiterated that same idea. But we are on this journey together; instead, I will offer you an important clue: Healing won't happen without first forming healthy relationships with your students.

Reflection

With the goal of fostering healthy, positive relationships with your students, I ask you to reflect on the following.

In your mind's eye, try to visualize three students in your classroom, one at a time. In particular, visualize their faces. With these images and associations in mind, ask yourself the following questions with respect to each of these students:

- What do I know about my student? What else do I need to know?
- Do I recognize my student's unique strengths and talents? If so, what are they?
- Have I ever communicated that I recognize and acknowledge these gifts during my interactions with this student?
- What can I do to help my student build on their strengths and realize their full potential?

Now, give consideration to how you felt as you responded to these questions. If, like many of us, you experienced discomfort, perhaps in the form of shame or guilt, remember your Radical Self-Care toolbox—the closest we'll get to an actual bag of tricks. Remind yourself that shame is rarely an effective motivator—for you or your students—and is not the premise of this work. Remind yourself that by engaging in this humbling yet also healing work, it is *within your power* to begin to reverse the harm perpetrated by an inequitable education system and a society that serves to diminish the humanity of not only the three students you visualized, but all people with marginalized identities.

Often, our students have been taught by teachers who didn't believe in their ability to prove their genius, to demonstrate student leadership, to engage in rigorous instruction, and to critically analyze ideas and policies. They have missed out on the joy of learning. They have missed out on engaging in caring relationships with teachers and other students. Teachers have missed out on the healthy experiences that help their students grow into people who not only realize their potential but can also improve their communities and the world. This vision of social justice and giving back to one's community has always been a core concept and intended outcome of culturally responsive teaching (Ladson-Billings, 1994). Later in this chapter, we'll explore an important conceptual extension of culturally responsive teaching—culturally sustaining pedagogy, a body of work that aims to reinforce the value and beauty of one's home culture and language. But first, we will consider some of the common barriers to healing and liberation.

Healing will never take place until we recognize, acknowledge, and take action to repair past and present harms. Take a moment to think about the policies and practices at work in your school and district that have created barriers to the formation of positive student identities and, ultimately, student achievement. Here are a few to consider:

- Overreliance on a single data point (the results of standardized tests) as a measure of students' abilities and capacities as well as the value of one's teaching (Safir & Dugan, 2021)
- Inequitable grading policies and practices (Feldman-Maggor et al., 2024)—why shouldn't our students be afforded opportunities for revisions before a grade is finalized?
- Failure to attend to and meet the needs of the whole child. The reform policies of the NCLB era virtually ignored the affective domain, such as a child's sense of safety and belonging, and

focused exclusively on cognitive measures. Any teacher (or parent) will tell you that a child is more than the sum of their test scores. Why is it that it took a devastating pandemic to convince parents, administrators, and policymakers that brain health really matters (Hettleman, 2005)?

- Zero-tolerance disciplinary policies that feed the playground-to-prison pipeline (Milner et al., 2018)
- Systemic tracking of students by perceived ability levels (Fergus, 2017; Oakes, 2005)
- At the classroom level, holding diminished expectations for historically underserved students and suppressing the cognitive and intellective capacity of these students by denying them access to rigorous instruction and learning (Emdin, 2016; Hammond, 2015)

While the harm inflicted by these barriers runs deep, think of them as symptoms of a greater systemic failure—a system that was designed to serve one group of children at the expense of others. When we begin to examine the "way we do school" through a racialized lens, we can fully appreciate author and scholar Bettina Love's (2023) statement that we transform education by "uprooting racism, sexism, homophobia, transphobia, and other forms of discrimination; eliminating structural barriers that have historically excluded people of color, queer folx, disabled folx, and women."

While some prefer to think of racism (and other isms) as individual traits of "bad people," Love emphasizes that they are actually systems of oppression that have an impact on *all* people. She further explains that focusing on such forms of systemic discrimination allows us to "create school climates where all students' families and educators feel welcome, supported, and valued"; she goes on to emphasize that "ensuring that students from all backgrounds and abilities have what they need to excel while understanding students whose families have survived racism and anti-Blackness for centuries—this will require additional resources" (2023, p. 285).

Love's (2023) comprehensive analysis of the policies and changes from *Brown v. Board of Education* to contemporary school reform measures, presents the trajectory of decisions that contributed to the systemic harm of our students. Unfortunately, the majority of these policies failed to honor the humanity of our students—a group that now comprises the largest segment of our public school students—nor did they improve their experiences of schooling for these students. Moreover, many of these same policies also harmed educators and devalued the teaching profession by attempting to apply business models to this most human of the human services. Think about it: Schools, unlike Fortune 500 corporations, are grounded in human interactions and relationships. Reflect on the visualization activity you just completed; when you concentrated on visualizing your students' faces, did you immediately flash to their scores on norm-referenced standardized tests? Although some students certainly benefited from these reform policies (particularly those with the means to afford outside assistance, such as tutoring, and those whose home cultures mirrored the commonly accepted cultural norms of the school), the so-called "achievement gaps" that these policies promised to close, failed to narrow. Teachers and school leaders during the No Child Left Behind Era were so preoccupied with chasing the elusive gain of high-stakes test scores that it was easy to lose sight of our students, multilingual learners, students with IEPs, and those from low-income households who grew increasingly disengaged from the endless worksheets and "flavor of the week" remediation programs that were implemented without consideration of their needs. Similarly, classroom teachers grew increasingly disillusioned from those initiatives, the heavily scripted curriculum, and taking the heat for a host of systemic failings.

Bettina Love's conclusion that "the reform movement over the last 40 years is rooted in the ongoing harm of children of color" (2023) signals the urgency for a new paradigm to replace the dehumanizing, inequitable system we have lived with for far too long. Love proposes that we begin with *reparations* that "make real and tangible what a group has lost as a result of unequal access and treatment." For educators, healing can only take place when we become conscious of how our own decisions and actions can help or harm the students we serve. You have, no doubt, heard the expression that "Fish don't know they're in water." It's a good metaphor for understanding how those of us who have grown up and have been enculturated into a system that is inherently oppressive, unjust, and dehumanizing have come to accept and even embrace the norms of that system. In the process, although we may have been well-intentioned, we may have actually caused harm to the students under our care, as well as to ourselves. Again, I urge you to think of your journey to becoming a Warm Demander Teacher as a journey of healing, repair, and liberation.

Healing is best achieved when it takes place in community, yet in many schools, teachers work in relative isolation. When you, together with the entire school community, embark on a collaborative journey toward healing and liberation, everybody benefits. Best of all, the results are tangible. Warm Demander Teachers who have put in the time and emotional labor to examine and shift erroneous beliefs and understand how these beliefs are formed and strengthened by a toxic system, gain the power to reverse the harms that have endured through generations. In the process, you will regain your wholeness, health, freedom, and joy that accompanies teaching highly engaged, motivated, and self-directed learners.

Reflection

Pause and breathe. Visualize each of your students functioning at their highest potential (Walker, 1995).

- What are the sights and sounds that surface in such spaces?
- What are the signs that a student is highly engaged?
- Think about the conversations that are taking place between your students, between you and your students. How are these students leading? How are they self-directing their own learning? And how are they experiencing joy? (Muhammad, 2023)
- How do you feel as you imagine this scenario?

Pause and breathe again. Visualize your present classroom.

- Is it a place of excitement, empowerment, and joy?
- Are there observable signs that your students are engaged?
- What are the conversations that are enacted in this space?

If there is gap between your first (idealized) and second (real) visualizations, take comfort in the fact that you are not alone, but more importantly, it is within your power to close this gap. Warm Demander Teachers start to create these conditions by seeing and respecting the humanity of students. Beneath my request to visualize the faces of your three students is a call to humanize them. Such humanization lays the groundwork for the formation of healthy and healing relationships. Stop and breathe again as you consider what is required to achieve this change and the gifts you and your students will receive from that transformation.

Transformative Personal and Student Relationships

Researchers and practitioners of culturally responsive education agree that healthy and positive relationships are critical aspects of academic achievement for our students' well-being. Once again, I turn to the lessons learned from the generations of Black teachers who actively practiced critical care (Rolón-Dow, 2005) and were fully attuned to the delicate balance between warm, loving support and the fussiness that calls upon students to meet high expectations, engage in productive struggle (Hammond, 2015), and ultimately become leaders of their own learning (Emdin, 2016). Again, while Black and BIPOC teachers may have a more culturally intuitive grasp of Warm Demander pedagogy, by no means do I believe that achieving such proficiency in such skills is unattainable for any teacher. It is certainly within reach, but it requires a fair amount of personal well-being, cultural humility, self-awareness, critical consciousness, and practice.

Kristen E. Duncan (2022) provides an exceptional examination on the historical pedagogy and motivation of Black teachers in an extensive review, starting with Reconstruction (Anderson, 1988) and continuing through Jim Crow legislation, where Black teachers saw their job as "collective racial uplift" (Walker, 1996). Duncan provides multiple examples of culturally responsive and healing strategies by historic and contemporary Black teachers that focus positive attention and care on their students. These teachers supported racial justice as they *saw themselves* in their students, a common theme in the culturally responsive teaching literature (Foster, 1997; Ladson-Billings, 1994; Walker, 1995), and they created familial or communal classrooms. These teachers embraced the role of surrogate parents, such as other mothers (Ware, 2006), who affirmed their students and validated their knowledge. They also directly and explicitly discussed race and racism and created safe spaces for students.

Black teachers were fully cognizant of the need to openly address issues of race with their students. To have avoided or ignored such topics was seen as a failure of their responsibility to Black students (Dixson, 2003; Lynn & Jennings, 2009; Milner et al., 2016). By surfacing and discussing these stark realities, students will learn effective coping mechanisms and, most importantly, find ways to challenge them. These teachers saw it as "their job" (Duncan, 2022, p. 1) to give students the tools to navigate white supremacy and maintained an obligation to help disprove the myth that Black students were inferior.

Relationships don't take place in a vacuum. They are impacted by the greater ecosystem, including societal forces that impact us for better or worse. Recall that a key distinction between "care" and "critical care" in the context of teaching is race consciousness that is grounded in an historical understanding of how these societal forces disproportionately affected peoples' lives (Rolón-Dow, 2005). Healing doesn't take place by denying the presence of harm. Such denial won't engender trust from your students, nor will it counteract the damaging effects of deficit narratives.

As we see from Duncan (2022), conversations about race are not avoided by teachers and administrators who are committed to improving education for our students. In fact, the disruption of racism motivated teachers who engaged in emancipatory pedagogy to counter the narrative that pathologized Black students. The author states,

> Embracing emancipatory pedagogy would not only lead teachers to helping their students achieve their academic goals, but it would also help them understand the systemic and structural barriers that students of color face both in and out of schools. While it may be unrealistic to expect every teacher in the U.S. to be able to engage students in the exact ways these teachers have, it would not be impossible for the majority of teachers to move in this direction. (Duncan, 2022, p. 15)

Think back to what means to "see ourselves" in our students. It should come as no surprise that teachers who share the racial identities of their historically underserved students and have, themselves, encountered marginalization, microaggressions, deficit narratives, and other invalidation have unique insight into the lived experiences of their students. They also have a willingness to be vulnerable and, when appropriate, share their own experiences navigating racist systems. Duncan offers the example of a Black male teacher willing to be vulnerable with students when discussing the impact of "police violence and other issues that disproportionately affect Black students" (2022, p. 10). His readiness to show vulnerability and share his stories and his pain with students demonstrates how adults can feel deeply about various experiences and exemplifies how a relationship that builds trust can create student achievement. This example also demonstrates how heartfelt transparency between teachers with students can help both teachers and students focus on their mutual humanity. Students also learn the dynamics of caring and healthy relationships. One can see how such nuanced relationships naturally support engaging pedagogy and brain healthy environments (Hammond, 2015), allowing students to see themselves as successful learners and members of a caring community.

Such educators share the goal of not "saving" their students, but equipping them with the tools, counternarratives, and understandings that help counteract the ill effects of living in a racist society. If you ever find yourself feeling that your job is to save or "rescue" the children under your care, it's time for a cognitive reboot. Replace the "save" with words like "empower," "identify skills," and "discover talent." And remind yourself that your students have already accomplished the remarkable feat of surviving a system that failed to affirm or value them. And they deserve a better experience.

Admittedly, teachers who do not share the students' racial identity may need to work harder to win the trust of their students—a trust that is the foundation of positive relationships. If this feels at all insurmountable, remind yourself that you don't have to do it alone. Remember, *healing is best accomplished when it takes place in community.* You have much to gain by engaging in conversations with other educators who share your commitment to removing oppressive barriers and healing from the toxic effects of racist, inequitable institutions. Your Warm Demander peers also share the knowledge that *they are also harmed* by perpetuating a system that incarcerates not only their students' imaginations but their own (Safir & Dugan, 2021). In turn, their healing is transformational to their relationship with students. These are critical aspects to building our students' trust, and all contribute to developing a successful student-learner identity. There is an example from Ms. Davis's class that will illustrate this trust later in the chapter.

Consider the importance of relationships that are built on trust, relationships that position your students to thrive. How can a Warm Demander Teacher intentionally build such relationships and become aware of whether their actions have earned their students' trust. What are the indicators of trust, and how does a Warm Demander Teacher intersect with those indicators?

To build trust, talk with your students. Notice if you experience fear in engaging in thoughtful conversations about trust. Ask them what they see as examples of trust. Consider the potential for a lack of cultural synchronization (Irvine, 1990) regarding your beliefs and their beliefs of what behaviors create trust. Use the following chart to document and engage in reflective practice (Cadray, 1999) as you have conversations with your students and to reflect on lessons. Consider that relationships are built throughout the day, including during instruction, and as you co-create and maintain classroom culture.

Reflective Practice Activity for Building Relationships

To explore healing relationships and building with students, thoughtfully reflect and write examples of relationship-building activities and indicators of a relationship that is focused on and supportive of students.

RELATIONSHIP BUILDERS	RELATIONSHIP INDICATORS
Example: While students are talking, the teacher maintains eye contact and a facial expression of interest. When responding to the student, the teacher repeats to clarify understanding of the students' comments. The teacher continues with comments such as, "I appreciate your ideas," "I had not thought of it that way," and "I think that is a brilliant conclusion."	***Example:*** Students, in turn, demonstrate they've received the teacher's encouragement through their relaxed body language. They listen with interest and smile or act as though they are proud. The student and/or classmates might clap or cheer at the positive feedback from the teacher acknowledging the student taught the teacher a new idea.

RELATIONSHIP BUILDERS	RELATIONSHIP INDICATORS
Your Example:	*Your Example:*
______________	______________
______________	______________
______________	______________
______________	______________
______________	______________
______________	______________
______________	______________
______________	______________
______________	______________
______________	______________

These activities call for deep reflection, particularly for teachers who don't share the cultural identities of their students. At the same time, your responses to the prompts can become the foundation for engaging in transformational relationships with your students. If you are stymied by the belief that forming such relationships is beyond your reach, remind yourself that it can and has been done (Emdin, 2016). And remind yourself that you must try. You might start by seeking opportunities to observe and/or collaborate with other teachers who exhibit Warm Demander traits and have earned the trust of their students. Again, talk with your students. You can ask them to talk about their favorite teachers—past and present—and how these teachers supported, encouraged, even inspired them. If you approach these conversations with genuine curiosity, interest, and a fair degree of cultural humility, you will not only gain valuable insights into their lived experiences, interests, and passions, but you may also begin to earn their trust.

As you build trust and you have a class that can actively engage in conversations about race, think back to the identity work you did earlier in the book. Just as you have worked on developing your own positive cultural/racial identity, encouraging students to have a positive cultural/racial identity makes discussing race a healthier conversation. Of course, your students take a risk when they become vulnerable enough to share their experiences with you and their peers. It takes courage, just as it takes courage on your part to make the space for race conversations with your students. It also takes practice: rehearse active listening skills with a trusted friend. When you become comfortable with being an active listener, model it for your students during conversations and during instruction. In the course of your instruction, they should frequently engage in active listening in pair-share dyads. Above all, remember that critical care entails understanding how a child is impacted by society. What better way to learn than to listen to your students as they share their experiences (both good and bad), opinions, passions, and hopes? In association with the "one small thing, done consistently" strategy we learned in our Radical Self-Care work, I encourage teachers to work on developing one behavior at a time as you grow your critical care with our students. Always be your authentic self—one that demonstrates love to the students, as well as commitment to seeing them thrive. When they see your commitment to them thriving, that supports their trust in you. Essential to Warm Demander teaching is a commitment to students not merely surviving the school experience but thriving as a result of your actions.

With careful examination and reflection, you will identify actions and strategies to strengthen your relationships and support your students in countering the learned helplessness that is a casualty of repeatedly being told that they will never be good enough (Hammond, 2015). They will in turn, through their own efforts and talents, discredit the low expectations of people who presume African, African American, Asian Pacific Islanders, Black, Chicano, differently abled, Hispanic, Indigenous, Latino/a, and LGBTQIA+ students are incapable of academic achievement or success in life. Warm Demander Teachers who intentionally help students to create a successful student-learner identity that supports academic growth can create reciprocal relationships that achieve the synergy of students' intellectual and leadership growth and teacher–student transformation.

Creating Successful Student-Learner Identities

As emphasized earlier in this chapter, your own healing will ultimately contribute to your ability to promote the healing of your students. Healing from deficit narratives and other manifestations of racism and oppression liberates you and your students. The sense of success and well-being that you experience as your students begin to fly will contribute to your own formation of a positive teacher identity. You become more adept at identifying the brilliance in every student and communicating your belief in them. Such positive affirmation can help promote your students' liberation from the devaluation and dehumanizing byproducts of racism, such as learned helplessness and "stereotype threat," a barrier that you will learn more about later in this chapter (Steele, 2011). They will form more positive learner identities as their sense of safety, belonging, and self-efficacy increases. Those with positive learner identities have the capacity to meet more challenging academic demands. As you become more skilled at the delicate dance between administering loving support, being the leader of the class, and the fussiness that may seem to drive your students crazy (but, in actuality, drives them to exceed your highest expectations), together you will be able to envision a better, more just, and healing world.

Culturally Sustaining Pedagogy

Culturally sustaining pedagogy (or CSP) builds on the assets-based frameworks of culturally responsive teaching by emphasizing the importance of not only affirming the cultural heritage of students and families but also intentionally committing to *preserve* students' home cultures and languages as a part of schooling for social transformation in a pluralistic society. Authors and scholars Django Paris (2012) and H. Samy Alim (2017) have made a significant contribution to this important body of theory and practice. In their words, "In our work with CSP, we begin . . . with the knowledge that our languages, literacies, histories and cultural ways of being as people and communities of color are not pathological" (Paris & Alim, 2017, p. 2).

The concept of culturally sustaining pedagogy highlights positive social transformation and respects cultural dexterity. The authors underscore the importance of the latter: Pedagogies can and should teach students to be linguistically and culturally flexible across multiple language varieties and cultural ways of believing and interacting:

> We are committed to envisioning and enacting pedagogies that are not filtered through the glass of amused contempt and pity
>
> *(Continued)*

(Continued)

. . . but rather are centered on contending in complex ways with the rich and innovative linguistic, literate, and cultural practices of Indigenous, Black, Latinx, Asian, Pacific Islander and other youth and communities of color. (Paris & Alim, 2017, p. 2)

CSP seeks to disrupt deficit narratives that pathologize children and families with those that celebrate their funds of knowledge (Moll et al., 1992) and ample linguistic and cultural gifts. It supports multilingualism and multiculturalism as a pluralistic society needs many and one to remain vibrant (Paris, 2012).

Culturally sustaining pedagogy offers a powerful counternarrative to subtractive and deficit-based practices. Warm Demander Teachers appreciate the significance and value of cultural and linguistic sustainability and work to further it in their curriculum and instruction. These actions provide another pathway to healing relationships that affirm and celebrate our students' cultural and linguistic identities. They also fuel the development of positive learner identities by challenging the trope that BIPOC students and multilingual learners lack the knowledge and skills to be held to rigorous academic standards. CSP honors and serves to sustain the wealth of cultural knowledge skills students bring into schools and builds upon them in a way that exceeds earlier frameworks and models of culturally responsive teaching.

Being a Hard/Easy Teacher

Warm Demander Teachers have shared variations of the same story of talking to their students about their talents or sharing with students their belief in their ability to learn the content. As teachers worked to change students' self-affirmation (Cohen & Sherman, 2014; Steele, 1988) or create neuroplasticity (Achor, 2010), they demonstrated pedagogy that helped students who did not believe in themselves become successful.

Ms. Davis had a student whose academic engagement had been low at the beginning of the quarter. He believed the content was too difficult and the teacher's expectations too high. In response, Ms. Davis did not lower her expectations for the student to complete the assignments successfully or accept his beliefs about his limited capacity. Further, despite the differences in their socioeconomic status, race, and gender, the teacher did not let those factors be a limitation. At the end of the quarter, the student complimented the teacher by telling her she was a ***hard/ easy teacher.*** Additionally, Ms. Davis, a white teacher, achieved this success by being a Warm Demander Teacher consistent with her quiet personality.

In other words, the subject matter and the expectations for completing the content were harder than the student believed within his abilities. However, the teacher's beliefs about the student's talents, which were demonstrated through her consistent instruction and expectations, made it possible for him to learn despite his initial beliefs and resistance. Ms. Davis's show of loving support transformed his learner identity, setting him free to fly academically.

In Christoper Emdin's book *For White Folks Who Teach in the Hood,* he reminds us, "If we are truly interested in transforming schools and meeting the needs of urban youth of color who are the most disenfranchised within them, educators must create safe and trusting environments that are respectful of student's culture" (2016, p. 27). Throughout this book, you have been reminded that far too many of our students experience multiple negative messages and judgments that undermine the formation of positive learner identities. When you allow yourself the freedom to listen to your students' race conversations, examples of these messages are sure to surface. The collective weight of negative messages, compounded by traumatic life experiences in school and beyond, contribute to what you may perceive as resistance and lack of trust. Warm Demander Teachers who consistently work to heal the harm of such oppression by offering affirmation and encouragement to students (Matthews, 2020) just *don't give up,* despite the protestations of their students that a task is beyond their abilities. In such instances, the Warm Demander's resilience contributes to the student's resilience, which in turn allows the student to remain in the zone of productive struggle, take on increasingly demanding academic work, and believe in their capacity to learn and achieve.

I've come across numerous anecdotal pieces of evidence to support the power of affirming students' abilities and talents in the formation of more positive learning identities, as well as the evidence in research studies. Borman et al. (2015) found measurable improvements in cumulative grade point averages for racial/ethnic minority students through an intervention of self-affirmation through expressive writing (Liu & Steele, 1986; Steele, 1988; Steele & Liu, 1983). Stereotype threat research attributes opportunity gaps to the common fear among BIPOC and other marginalized people that those in dominant majority will hold negative stereotypes with respect to their academic and other abilities (Steele & Aronson, 1995). Such fears among students can lead to self-fulling prophecies that their academic performance doesn't accurately reflect their capacities. Some common examples include the systemic undermining of performance for "African Americans and Hispanics in academic subjects or women in mathematics" (Borman et al., 2015). In the research conducted by Borman et al., an intervention designed to help students affirm their own strengths and abilities in writing also demonstrates the power of neuroplasticity (Anchor, 2010). Yes, being reminded of their own brilliance and affirming it yourself in well-designed assignments can actually help rewire students' brains in a manner that helps them overcome fears of failure, become better learners, and, more generally, better versions of themselves.

In summary, Warm Demander Teachers realize they have the simultaneous tasks of removing students' deficit beliefs and replacing them with asset-based beliefs about their abilities and talents, a successful learner identity. Sometimes the removal of deficit beliefs occurs through explicit conversations; other times it is achieved through engaging instruction and your own resilience and tenacity to help students succeed, as demonstrated by Ms. Davis. Our students need both types of Warm Demander Teacher behaviors. This mindset shift is more easily attained by teachers who have engaged in Radical Self-Care and experienced for themselves the ways to rewire their brain, such as identifying and eliminating the inner critic, removing internalized racism, or creating new, healthy habits. The knowledge of how to activate neuroplasticity can easily lead to creating a welcoming and "brain safe" (Hammond, 2015) classroom environment that contributes to healing and learning for students and teachers.

On Matters of the Heart

As you now understand, becoming a Warm Demander Teacher is layered, complex, and achievable. It is *not* a detached intellectual pursuit that leads to performative behaviors, but rather an inherently messy but heartfelt and rewarding endeavor. Responding to the commitment to be a Warm Demander Teacher starts with your heart and requires a ***willingness*** to care deeply about students who have been failed by years of education systems and are owed an educational debt (Ladson-Billings, 2006).

A teacher's heart recognizes the humanity of our students, responds to their desire to be treated humanely, encourages them to show their talents, and lovingly pushes them into a successful learner-identity. Additionally, your heart drives you and others to shed the deficit-based biases that are the biproduct of a racist society. Teachers who teach from the heart are not only aware of how perpetuating such biases hurts their students but also how it hurts their own hearts. Remind yourself that the heart work that I have called upon you to do is also healing work for you. Remind yourself it's worth the time, the emotional labor, and the risk to rekindle the mission, the passion, the purposeful work, and the love that brought you into this profession in the first place. Remind yourself that it is within your power to help heal a broken world.

Warm Demander teaching can liberate you, as it was born out of the liberatory practices of teachers that started with Reconstruction. The lessons learned from the work of Black teachers from the time of the Reconstruction to the present, Black teachers who have challenged deficit narratives, beat odds of "predictable failure," and helped their students fly in the face of systemic injustice, hardship, and trauma have convinced me that *all* teachers hold the power to disrupt oppression in schools and society. I also continue to believe healing is best done in a community, and I encourage you to build your community with like-minded educators who are ***willing*** to become Warm Demander Teachers.

If you, like most teachers, believe in the power of learning, the inherent goodness and value of humanity, and the possibility of a better future for your students, it is in your power to reimagine and change the narrative.

Closing Note: Envisioning a New World

Author and scholar Shawn Ginwright (2022) offers insightful strategies to reimagine our lives, our interactions with each other, and, ultimately, our schools. He tells us that creating the kinds of transformations that I propose throughout this book are only difficult to imagine because we have experienced inequity, and that harm limits our imagination:

> Inequality erodes our ability to imagine any other way, and it conditions us to only focus on surface solutions to deep problems. It pre-defines our dreams and dictates what we can imagine. That's why so many of us have a hard time describing what freedom feels, looks, smells, and sounds like. (p. 7)

Ginwright (2022) continues his observation that we spend so much time fighting symptoms or indicators of oppression that we spend less time producing the transformation we desire through **creating, cultivating, inventing, and designing**.

Reflective Practice Activity

Write a reflection on the meaning of these words:

- Create: ______________________________

  ____

- Cultivate: ______________________________

  ____

- Invent: ______________________________

  ____

- Design: ______________________________

  ____

Consider the meaning of these words as you imagine a new system of education, one that values justice and the inherent humanity of all students—one that values the profession of teaching and supports practitioners in their desire to serve all students.

Now imagine how you and your students experience this new normal.

In Ginwright's acclaimed book *The Four Pivots: Reimagining Justice, Reimagining Ourselves* (2022), I found in "Pivot Two, From Transactional to Transformative" a clear parallel to my vision for Warm Demander

Teachers. Contemplating the transformation of teachers, students, and classrooms, he proposed that we cultivate a "new world perspective and power" in which we focus on the depths of our relationships and quality of our vision. In its implementation, we create a beloved community that fosters an authentic sense of belonging and relationships with people who are outside the community that we were born into. He further proposes that we pivot into healing and caring communities that will cultivate transformative relationships.

Dare I propose that too much of education has been transactional and not transformative? Think back to Bettina Love's conclusion that the reform movement over the last 40 years is rooted in the ongoing harm of children of color. The surface-level, technical fixes of our post *Brown* school reform efforts have, for the most part, been informed by deficit thinking. Even the word "reform" implies that we must work within the existing system to effect change. What happens when we substitute words like "disrupt" and "replace" for reform? This subtle shift in language signals a major shift from transactional to transformative. Finally, think about this: The very notion of a silver bullet or a bag of tricks is antithetical to the idea of deep-seated change. Our profession is fraught with complexity, and the reductionist, cause-and-effect reasoning that is at the heart of most reform efforts has done little to advance us.

Even culturally responsive teaching has been misrepresented, misconstrued, and frequently implemented in a superficial, inauthentic manner. Teachers who thought they could hook their students into lessons simply by adding the *music du jour* to their instruction abandoned their efforts to impart cultural relevance when they realized that this surface-level change alone wouldn't raise test scores, nor would it magically create happily engaged students with strong learner identities. In doing so, they missed the opportunity to transform their relationships as well as promote deeper levels of learning for their students. How might we take such a transactional approach to the realm of the transformational beyond merely changing our music? Imagine a lesson that calls upon students to engage in a critical analysis of their favorite song, beginning with articulating their personal connection to it. Imagine amplifying this lesson even more by asking a student how this song reflects (or perhaps doesn't reflect) their lived experience and culture. Such a lesson is not only student-centered but is indicative of care and healing in that it works to sustain and value the students and culture. In this scenario, you have the opportunity to demonstrate your care and strengthen their trust by listening with cultural humility and showing authentic curiosity. And in this scenario, your students have the opportunity to demonstrate their capacity to lead a discussion on the topic and create questions that challenge their fellow students to consider new ideas, lovingly disagree with one another, and experience joy.

Your students deserve to heal. Your students deserve to fly. And you have the power to help them do just that.

I'd like to conclude this chapter with a quote from Ms. Carter, whom you may recall from previous chapters. Ms. Carter was one of the teachers who participated in my 2006 Warm Demander research and one who believes that we all have the power to undo past harm and effect true transformation. She stated,

> What we know is that before *Brown v. Board of Education*, 25% of the nation's teachers were Black teachers who were teaching Black students. Now, in 2023, well after segregation and systemic policies that restrict authentic learning and increase standardized assessments, only about 8% of this nation's teachers are Black. The system has been built so that children of color and the oppressed people from marginalized communities do not succeed by not providing them a fair and equitable education. The answer to that is to increase the number of teachers of color, who believe they are teaching human beings and not numbers.
>
> Do you have to be an advocate to be a teacher? Yes. The heart [of teaching] is to be a human being and to see children as human beings. Research tells us we can become academically successful when our teachers believe in us. We must have people who have that heart. That heart is understanding that people make money off education. They make money off standardized testing. . . . The people who had a heart for working with and changing things for those students, they've taken them out of the mix. . . . That heart is knowing who you are as a person and knowing that you are there to change the system and that's where the efficacy comes from. It's more than just a heart, it is

> a heart of love. But it's a heart of courage. It is a heart of "I'm not going to ignore all these Black children in this building that have all this talent and potential."
>
> I was reading a primary document about one of the first Black schools in South Carolina.
>
> They were enslaved, they were teaching Black males reading and how to be literate before 1865 . . . free Black people also came to the South to teach, I know men were doing it as well as women. We need to bring them all back. The strength of us is in coming back together and bringing Black men back into education.
>
> To be a Warm Demander, you have to be willing to advocate, and you have to be willing and ready to fight. White teachers can be Warm Demanders; they must be co-conspirators, more than allies, they need to be more than people who just float in. When Bree Newsome climbed that flagpole, there was a white man holding the pole for her—as we know there have been white people who have been ready for the fight.

Being a Warm Demander is being an advocate and an ally. It's true that we have lost too many gifted Black educators post *Brown* and into the present. Irvine's (2003) classic scholarship recommended that we work to diversify the teaching population, and that recommendation has not lost its importance based on national teacher shortages (Craig et al., 2023). Yet Irvine also observed that "increasing the number of teachers of color does not, in any way, imply devaluing white teachers. A diversified teaching force makes for a strong and effective teaching corps" (2003, p. 61). Schools need Warm Demander Teachers that have the heart to care and love, to encourage, inspire, challenge, learn from, laugh with, lead, and be led by our students. We need teachers to become Warm Demander Teachers, and we need other teachers to expand their Warm Demander Teacher skills. We need all of you to make schools welcoming to teachers who will support the diverse population of students in schools. We need teachers with hearts for their students to make the hard work attainable and to teach them to fly.

References

Achor, S. (2010). *The happiness advantage: How a positive brain fuels success in work and life.* Currency.

Achor, S. (2011, May). The happy secret to better work. [Video]. TEDx. Bloomington.

Adeeyo, O. (2022). *Self-care for Black women: 150 ways to radically accept and prioritize your mind, body, and soul.* Simon & Schuster.

Alexander, M. (2020). *The new Jim Crow: Mass incarceration in the age of colorblindness.* New Press.

Anderson, J. D. (1988). *The education of Blacks in the South, 1860–1935.* University of North Carolina Press.

Ariati, J., Pham, T. M., & Vogler, J. S. (2023). *Data from: Constructivist learning environments: Validating the community of inquiry survey for face-to-face contexts.* https://hdl.handle.net/11244/337149

Bailey, M. (2016). Misogynoir in medical media: On Caster Semenya and R. Kelly. *Catalyst: Feminism, Theory, Technoscience, 2*(2), 1–31.

Baldwin, J. (1963). The Negro child-his self-image. *The Saturday Review.*

Baldwin, J. (1980). Notes on the house of bondage. *The Nation.*

Bartolomé, L. (2008). Authentic cariño and respect in minority education: The political and ideological dimensions of love. *International Journal of Critical Pedagogy, 1*(1), 1–17.

Bonilla-Silva, E. (2022). Color-blind racism in pandemic times. *Sociology of Race and Ethnicity, 8*(3), 343–354.

Borman, G. D., Grigg, J., Rozek, C., & Hanselman, P. (2015). *The sustained effects of a brief self-affirmation intervention on students' academic outcomes across middle and high school.* Society for Research on Educational Effectiveness.

Bryant, J., Ram, S., Scott, D., & Williams, C. (2023). *K–12 teachers are quitting. What would make them stay?* McKinsey & Company. https://www.mckinsey.com/industries/education/our-insights/k-12-teachers-are-quitting-what-would-make-them-stay

Bryant-Davis, T. (2007). Healing requires recognition: The case for race-based traumatic stress. *The Counseling Psychologist, 35*(1), 135–143.

Cadray, J. (1999). *The field experiences handbook* [Unpublished manuscript]. Emory University, Atlanta, GA.

Cammarota, J., & Romero, A. (2006). A critically compassionate intellectualism for Latina/o students: Raising voices above the silencing in our schools. *Multicultural Education, 14*(2), 16–23.

Cerezo, R., Fernández, E., Amieiro, N., Valle, A., Rosário, P., & Núñez, J. C. (2019). Mediating role of self-efficacy and usefulness between self-regulated learning strategy knowledge and its use. *Revista de Psicodidáctica (English ed.), 24*(1), 1–8.

Chatterjee, R. (2018a). *The stress solution: The 4 steps to reset your body, mind, relationships, and purpose.* Penguin Random House.

Chatterjee, R. (2018b). *The 4 pillar plan: How to relax, eat, move, sleep your way to a longer, healthier life.* Penguin Random House.

Chatterjee, R. (2023, January 11). *Neuroscientist reveals the first thing you should do every morning for longevity.* Wendy Suzuki [Video]. YouTube. https://www.youtube.com/watch?v=0-89SYgIwuo

Cleage, P. (2009). *What looks like crazy on an ordinary day: A novel.* HarperCollins.

Cohen, G. L., & Sherman, D. K. (2014). The psychology of change: Self-affirmation and social psychological intervention. *Annual Review of Psychology, 65,* 333–371.

Craig, C. J., Hill-Jackson, V., & Kwok, A. (2023). Teacher shortages: What are we short of? *Journal of Teacher Education, 74*(3), 209–213.

Crenshaw, K. (1991). Race, gender, and sexual harassment. *Southern California Law Review, 65,* 1467.

Cross, W. E., Jr. (1991). *Shades of black: Diversity in African-American identity.* Temple University Press.

Davis, D., & Hook, J. (2019). Cultural humility: Conclusion to the special issue. *Journal of Psychology and Theology, 47*(3) 230–239.

Delpit, L. (1995). *Other people's children: Cultural conflict in the classroom.* The New Press.

Delpit, L. (2006). *Other people's children: Cultural conflict in the classroom* (2nd ed.). The New Press.

Delpit, L. (2012). *Multiplication is for white people: Raising expectations for other people's children.* The New Press.

DiAngelo, R. (2016). White fragility. *Counterpoints, 497,* 245–253.

Dixson, A. D. (2003). "Let's do this!": Black women teachers' politics and pedagogy. *Urban Education, 38*(2), 217–235.

Duncan, K. E. (2022). "That's my job": Black teachers' perspectives on helping Black students navigate white supremacy. *Race Ethnicity and Education, 25*(7), 978–996.

Emdin, C. (2016). *For white folks who teach in the hood and the rest of y'all too: Reality pedagogy and urban education.* Beacon Press.

Farrelly, D., Kaplin, D., & Hernandez, D. (2022). A transformational approach to developing cultural humility in the classroom. *Teaching of Psychology, 49*(2), 185–190.

Feldman-Maggor, Y., Tuvi-Arad, I., & Blonder, R. (2024). Navigating the online learning journey by self-regulation: Teachers as learners. *Computers & Education, 219,* 105074.

Fergus, E. (2017). *Solving disproportionality and achieving equity. A leader's guide to using data to change hearts and minds.* Corwin.

Foronda, C. A. (2020). Theory of cultural humility. *Journal of Transcultural Nursing, 31*(1), 7–12.

Foster, M. (1997). *Black teachers on teaching.* New Press.

Gallardo, M. (Ed.). (2014). *Developing cultural humility: Embracing race, privilege, and power.* Sage.

Ginwright, S. A. (2022). *The four pivots: Reimaginingjustice, reimagining ourselves.* North Atlantic Books.

Goleman, D. (1998). What makes a good leader? *Harvard Business Review, 76*(6), 93–102.

Goleman, D. (2011). *The brain and emotional intelligence: New insights.* More than sound.

Gupta, S. (2022). *12 weeks to a sharper you: A guided program build a better brain at any age.* Simon & Schuster.

Hammond, Z. (2015). *Culturally responsive teaching and the brain: Promoting authentic engagement and rigor among culturally and linguistically diverse students.* Corwin.

Heinz, M. (2015). Why choose teaching? An international review of empirical studies exploring student teachers' career motivations and levels of commitment to teaching. *Educational Research and Evaluation, 21*(3), 258–297.

Helms, J. E. (1995). *An update of Helm's White and people of color racial identity models* [Conference session]. Versions were presented at the Psychology and Societal Transformation Conference, University of Western Cape, South Africa, January 1994, and at a workshop titled "Helm's Racial Identity Theory," Annual Multicultural Winter Roundtable, Teachers College–Columbia University, New York, February 1994. Sage.

Hersey, T. (2022). *Rest is resistance: A manifesto*. Little Brown Spark.

Hettleman, K. (2004). The road to nowhere: The illusion and broken promises of special education in the Baltimore and other public school systems. *Education Week*.

Hill, M. T. (2022). *Heal your way forward: The co-conspirator's guide to an antiracist future*. Row House by OrangeSky Audio.

Hinton, E., & Cook, D. (2021). The mass criminalization of Black Americans: A historical overview. *Annual Review of Criminology, 4*, 261–286.

Hoffman, J., & Hoffman, J. (2004). *Learning racial identity development using human sculpture*. Sculpturing Race handout. Long Beach, CA.

Hollins, E. (1982). The Marva Collins story revisited: Implications for regular classroom instruction. *Journal of Teacher Education, 33*(1), 37–40.

hooks, b. (2001). Homeplace (a site of resistance). In J. Ritchie & K. Ronald (Eds.), *Available means: An anthology of women's rhetoric(s)*. University of Pittsburgh Press.

Howell, D., Norris, A., & Williams, K. (2019). Towards a black gaze theory: How Black female teachers make Black students visible. *Hillard/Sizemore Special Edition, 6*(1), 20–23.

Huberman, A. (2024, April 3). *Dr. Matthew Walker: The biology of sleep & your unique needs*. Huberman Lab Guest Series [Video]. YouTube. https://www.youtube.com/watch?v=-OBCwiPPfEU

Irvine, J. J. (1990). *Black students and school failure. Policies, practices, and prescriptions*. Greenwood Press.

Irvine, J. J. (2003). *Educating teachers for diversity: Seeing with a cultural eye*. Teachers College Press.

Irvine, J. J. (Ed.). (2002). *In search of wholeness: African American teachers and their culturally specific classroom practices*. Palgrave.

Irvine, J. J., & Armento, B. J. (2001). Culturally responsive teaching: Lesson planning for elementary and middle grades. *Education Review*. httpJs://doi.org/10.14507/er.v0.177

Irvine, J. J., & Fraser, J. (1998, May 13). Warm Demanders: Do national certifications leave room for the culturally responsive pedagogy of African American teachers? *Education Week*, p. 56.

Kempf, A. (2022). Toward deeper unconscious racial bias work in education. *Teachers College Record, 124*(11), 3–29.

Kendi, I. X. (2016). *Stamped from the beginning: The definitive history of racist ideas in America*. Public Affairs.

Kendi, I. X. (2023). *How to be an antiracist*. OneWorld.

Kleinfeld, J. (1975). Effective teachers of Eskimo and Indian students. *The University of Chicago Press, 83*(2), 301–344.

Ladson-Billings, G. (1994). *The dreamkeepers: Successful teachers of African American students*. Jossey-Bass.

Ladson-Billings, G. (2006). From the achievement gap to the education debt: Understanding achievement in U.S. schools. *Educational Researcher, 35*(7), 3–12.

Ladson-Billings, G. (2021). Three decades of culturally relevant, responsive, & sustaining pedagogy: What lies ahead? *The Educational Forum, 85*(4), 351–354.

Liu, T. J., & Steele, C. M. (1986). Attributional analysis as self-affirmation. *Journal of Personality and Social Psychology, 51*(3), 531.

López, F. (2019). How educational settings inform Latino student identity and achievement. *Policy Insights From the Behavioral and Brain Sciences, 6*(2), 170–177.

Lorde, A. (1988). *A burst of light and other essays*. Firebrand Books.

Love, B. L. (2019). Dear white teachers: You can't love your Black students if you don't know them. *Education Week, 38*(26), 512–523.

Love, B. L. (2023). *Punished for dreaming: How school reform harms Black children and how we heal*. St. Martin's Press.

Lynn, M., & Jennings, M. E. (2009). Power, politics, and critical race pedagogy: A critical race analysis of Black male teachers' pedagogy. *Race Ethnicity and Education, 12*(2), 173–196.

Matias, C. E., & Liou, D. D. (2015). Tending to the heart of communities of color: Towards critical race teacher activism. *Urban Education, 50*(5), 601–625.

Matthews, J. S. (2020). Formative learning experiences of urban mathematics teachers' and their role in classroom care practices and student belonging. *Urban Education, 55*(4), 507–541.

McAllister, G. (2002). Multicultural professional development for African American teachers: The role of process-oriented models. In J. J. Irvine (Ed.), *In search of wholeness: African American teachers and their culturally specific classroom practices* (pp. 11–31). Palgrave.

Menakem, R. (2017). *My grandmother's hands*. Central Recovery Press.

Milner, H. R., IV. (2023). *The race card: Leading the fight for truth in America's schools*. Corwin.

Milner, H. R., IV, Cunningham, H. B., Delale-O'Connor, L., & Kestenberg, E. G. (2018). *"These kids are out of control": Why we must reimagine "classroom management" for equity*. Corwin.

Milner, H. R., IV, Delale-O'Connor, L. A., Murray, I. E., & Farinde, A. A. (2016). Reflections on Brown to understand *Milliken v. Bradley*: What if we are focusing on the wrong policy questions? *Teachers College Record, 118*(3), 1–32.

Moll, L. C., Amanti, C., Neff, D., & Gonzalez, N. (1992). Funds of knowledge for teaching using a qualitative approach to connect homes and classrooms. *Theory Into Practice, 31*(2), 132–141.

Moon, S. H., & Sandage, S. J. (2019). Cultural humility for people of color: Critique of current theory and practice. *Journal of Psychology and Theology, 47*(2), 76–86.

Morrison, T. (2020). https://www.thoughtco.com/toni-morrison-biography-3530577#:~:-text=Fast%20Facts%3A%20Toni%20Morrison&text=Notable%20Quote%3A%20%E2%80%9CIf%20you',confined%20by%20your%20own%20repression.%E2%80%9D

Muhammad, G. (2020). *Cultivating genus: An equity framework for culturally and historically responsive literacy*. Scholastic.

Muhammad, G. (2023). *A guide to culturally and historically responsive teaching and learning*. Scholastic.

Muhammad, G. E. (2018). A plea for identity and criticality: Reframing literacy learning standards through a four-layered equity model. *Journal of Adolescent & Adult Literacy, 62*(2), 137–142.

National Center for Education Statistics. (2023). Characteristics of public school teachers. *Condition of Education*. U.S. Department of Education, Institute of Education Sciences. https://nces.ed.gov/programs/coe/indicator/clr

Nichols, W. (2014). *Blue mind: The surprising science that shows how being near, in, or under water can make you happier, healthier, more connected, and better at what you do*. Little, Brown Spark.

Noddings, N. (1992). In defense of caring. *The Journal of Clinical Ethics, 3*(1), 15–18.

Oakes, J. (2005). *Keeping track: How schools structure inequality*. Yale University Press.

Oberle, E., & Schonert-Reichel, K. A. (2016). Stress contagion in the classroom? The link between classroom teacher burnout and morning cortisol in elementary school students. *Social Science and Medicine, 159*, 30–37.

Paris, D., & Alim, S. (Eds). (2017). *Culturally sustaining pedagogies: Teaching and learning for justice in a changing world*. Teachers College Press.

Paris, D. (2012). Culturally sustaining pedagogy: A needed change in stance, terminology, and practice. *Educational Researcher, 41*(3), 93–97.

Perry, A. M. (2019). *For better student outcomes, hire more Black teachers*. Brookings. https://www.brookings.edu/articles/for-better-student-outcomes-hire-more-black-teachers/

Pollock, M. (Ed.). (2008). *Everyday antiracism: Getting real about race in school*. The New Press.

Poston, W. C. (1990). The biracial identity development model: A needed addition. *Journal of Counseling & Development, 69*(2), 152–155.

Reynolds, J. (2017). *Long way down*. Simon and Schuster.

Riley, C. (2024). *Black liturgies: Prayers, poems, and meditations for staying human.* Convergent.

Roberts, D. (2021). *The new origin story: The 1691 project* (N. Hannah-Jones, Ed.) One World.

Rolón-Dow, R. (2005). Critical care: A color (full) analysis of care narratives in the schooling experiences of Puerto Rican girls. *American Educational Research Journal, 42*(1), 77–111.

Safir, S., & Dugan, J. (2021). *Street data: A next-generation model for equity, pedagogy, and school transformation.* Corwin.

Schhneider, B., Martinez, S., & Ownes, A. (2006). *Barriers to educational opportunities for Hispanics in the United States.* National Research Council. https://www.semanticscholar.org/paper/Barriers-to-Educational-Opportunities-for-Hispanics-Schhneider-Martinez/a69a6b7f14d97d6a4b20e39eb876d345a1788b63

Schwartz, K. (2019, December 18). How Ibram X. Kendi's definition of antiracism applies to schools. *KQED.* https://www.kqed.org/mindshift/54999/how-ibram-x-kendis-definition-of-antiracism-applies-to-schools

Singh, A. (2019). *The racial healing handbook: Practical activities to help you challenge privilege, confront systemic racism & engage in collective healing.* New Harbinger.

Singleton, G. (2015). *Courageous conversations about race: A field guide for achieving equity in schools.* Corwin.

Steele, C. M. (1988). The psychology of self-affirmation: Sustaining the integrity of the self. In L. Berkowitz (Ed.), *Advances in experimental social psychology* (Vol. 21, pp. 261–302). Academic Press.

Steele, C. M. (2011). *Whistling Vivaldi: How stereotypes affect us and what we can do.* W. W. Norton & Company.

Steele, C. M., & Aronson, J. (1995). Stereotype threat and the intellectual test performance of African Americans. *Journal of Personality and Social Psychology, 69*(5), 797.

Steele, C. M., & Liu, T. J. (1983). Dissonance processes as self-affirmation. *Journal of Personality and Social Psychology, 45*(1), 5.

Steele, D. M., & Cohn-Vargas, B. (2013). *Identity safe classrooms: Places to belong and learn.* Corwin.

Sue, D. W. (2015). *Race talk and the conspiracy of silence: Understanding and facilitating difficult dialogues on race.* John Wiley & Sons.

Suzuki, W. (2017, November). *The brain changing benefits of exercise.* [Video] TEDWomen.

Taie, S., Westat, L. L., & Merlin, J. (2023). *Results from the 2021–22 teacher follow-up survey to the National Teacher and Principal Survey: First look–summary report.* Institute of Educational Science, National Center for Education Statistics. https://nces.ed.gov/pubs2024/2024039SummaryM.pdf

Tatum, B. D. (2007). *Can we talk about race?: And other conversations in an era of school resegregation.* Beacon Press.

Tervalon, M., & Murray-Garcia, J. (1998). Cultural humility verses cultural competence: A critical distinction in defining physician training outcomes in multicultural education. *Journal of Health Care for the Poor and Underserved, 9*(2), 117–125.

Thurett, S. (2015, June). *You can grow new brain cells.* [Video]. TED@BCG London.

Utt, J., & Tochluk, S. (2020). White teacher, know thyself: Improving anti-racist praxis through racial identity development. *Urban Education, 55*(1), 125–152.

Vaidya, A. N., & Battey, D. (2022). Homeplace: Black teachers creating space for Black students in mathematics classrooms. *Teachers College Record, 124*(11), 218–256.

Valenzuela, A. (2002). Reflections on the subtractive underpinnings of education research and policy. *Journal of Teacher Education, 53*(3), 235–241.

Vasquez, J. A. (1988). Contexts of learning for minority students. *The Educational Forum, 52*(3), 243–253.

Vygotsky, L. S., & Cole, M. (1978). *Mind in society: Development of higher psychological processes.* Harvard University Press.

Walker, T. (2023). *Survey: Teachers work more hours per week than other working adults.* https://www.nea.org/nea-today/all-news-articles/

survey-teachers-work-more-hours-week-other-working-adults

Walker, V. S. (1995). *Their highest potential: An African American school community in the segregated south*. The University of North Carolina Press.

Walker, V. S. (2018). *The lost education of Horace Tate*. The New Press.

Walker-Barnes, C. (2023). *Sacred self-care: Daily practices for nurturing our whole selves*. HarperCollins.

Ware, F. (2006). Warm demander pedagogy: Culturally responsive teaching that supports a culture of achievement for African American students. *Urban Education, 41*, 427–456.

Ware, F. (2008). Culturally responsive constructivism: Creating a culture of achievement. *National Journal of Urban Education and Practice, 1*(4), 324–333.

Wilkerson, I. (2020). *Caste: The origins of our discontents*. Random House.

Zaccor, K. M. (2022). Connecting with students through a critical, participatory curriculum: An exploration into a high school history teacher's construction of teacher–student relationships. *Urban Education, 57*(5), 871–898.

Index

Helping educators make the greatest impact

CORWIN HAS ONE MISSION: to enhance education through intentional professional learning.

We build long-term relationships with our authors, educators, clients, and associations who partner with us to develop and continuously improve the best evidence-based practices that establish and support lifelong learning.

Zeitfracht Medien GmbH
Ferdinand-Jühlke-Straße 7
99095 Erfurt, Deutschland
produktsicherheit@kolibri360.de